THE LIFE AND ART OF MILDRED VALLEY THORNTON

The Unheralded Artists of BC — 4

THE LIFE AND ART OF
MILDRED VALLEY THORNTON

SHERYL SALLOUM

FOREWORD BY SHERRILL GRACE

MOTHER TONGUE PUBLISHING LIMITED
Salt Spring Island, B.C.
Canada

Library and Archives Canada Cataloguing in Publication

Salloum, Sheryl, 1950–

   The life and art of Mildred Valley Thornton / Sheryl Salloum.

(The unheralded artists of BC ; 4)

Includes bibliographical references and index.

ISBN 978–1–896949–05–5

   1. Thornton, Mildred Valley, 1890–1967. 2. Thornton, Mildred Valley, 1890–1967—Criticism and interpretation. 3. Painters—British Columbia--Biography. I. Title. II. Series: Unheralded artists of BC ; 4

ND249.F478F47 2010   759.11   C2011–901555–2

PREVIOUS SPREAD—
Chief Dan Cranmer, Nimpkish Tribe of the Kwakiutl at Alert Bay
1946, oil on board
30" x 22 "
IMAGE 16499,
COURTESY ROYAL
BC MUSEUM

〉 *Totem Poles, Hazelton*
n.d., watercolour
15" x 11"
PRIVATE COLLECTION
DAN FAIRCHILD PHOTOGRAPHY

Book design, layout and typesetting by Jan Westendorp
Typeset in Whitman—a typeface designed by Kent Lew—and URW Grotesk, designed by Hermann Zapf

All efforts have been made to locate copyright holders of source material wherever possible.

Printed and bound in Canada by Friesens
Printed on chlorine-free paper; inside pages are 10% PCW

Mother Tongue Publishing gratefully acknowledges the support of the Canada Council for the Arts, which last year invested $20.1 million in writing and publishing throughout Canada; the assistance of the Province of British Columbia through the B.C. Arts Council and the support of Anthony Westbridge of Westbridge Fine Art Gallery.

Nous remercions de son soutien le Conseil des Arts du Canada, qui a investi 20,1 millions de dollars l'an dernier dans les lettres et l'édition à travers le Canada.

Published by:

Mother Tongue Publishing Limited
290 Fulford-Ganges Road
Salt Spring Island, B.C. V8K 2K6
Canada
phone: 250–537–4155 fax: 250–537–4725

www.mothertonguepublishing.com

Represented in Canada by the Literary Press Group and distributed by LitDistCo in North America

In loving memory of my parents, John and Babe and Anne and Fred

The Touchwood Hills, circa 1930
oil on canvas, 30" x 36"
NATIONAL GALLERY OF CANADA
#16858
GIFT OF J.M. THORNTON, 1971
PHOTO © NATIONAL GALLERY OF CANADA

Contents

FOREWORD

*T*he Life and Art of Mildred Valley Thornton is a welcome addition to Mother Tongue's "The Unheralded Artists of BC" series, and I am grateful to Sheryl Salloum for bringing a forgotten artist to my attention. English-speaking Canada has rarely been kind to its artists, but we have many excellent artists to celebrate. The most famous of these people, from Margaret Atwood to Glenn Gould, Tom Thomson to Emily Carr, and more recently from Ken Lum to Joe Fafard and Leonard Cohen are well known and highly respected. They are translated and read world wide and are mythic figures with cult status internationally. Today the works of our best 20th-century painters fetch staggering prices at auction and enjoy retrospectives in major art galleries.

This has not always been the case. It is not that we had no writing, painting, or music a century ago, but that we saw ourselves as colonials who needed to import art; home-grown artists were believed to be of lesser value. Canadians, especially Anglophone Canadians, held a deep-seated suspicion of the arts: for religious or more practical reasons, art was considered frivolous, a potentially corrupting influence, and a waste of time when crops needed harvesting. British Columbia has been slower than most other provinces in abandoning frontier priorities. We have been slow to support the arts with provincial funding—Saskatchewan has a better record, not to mention Quebec—and in the early decades of the last century we had just begun to develop the infrastructure and audiences to support artistic activities.

Before World War Two, artists like Emily Carr were neglected, and after the war artists now recognized as major figures—Jack Shadbolt, E.J. Hughes, Maxwell Bates, for example—struggled against conservative attitudes and tastes to earn acceptance beyond the professional experts. Women artists had, and still have, additional obstacles to overcome that have little to do with ability and much to do with gender.

Thornton was seen by her contemporaries as a talented painter and an advocate for First Nations and for the arts. Her paintings sold and were cherished by their owners at a time when private art collecting in Canada was confined to a few wealthy individuals. Yet, in the years before her death in 1967, she could not place her collected works with any gallery. She was deemed to be a minor, rather dated, figural painter of marginal subjects. Canada has never *privileged* the figure in its pictures; landscape painting has been the dominant genre in representing the country. But Canadian artists have always painted the figure, and we have a marvellous collection of portraits spanning three centuries of artistic output.

Just as the portrait, the figure and First Nations subjects were not seen as sufficiently modern, the style in which Thornton painted was also seen by the fine arts community of the 1950s and 1960s to be out of date. Her work is representational—not narrowly documentary and mimetic, but clearly recognizable as pictures of places, faces and working life. She is not really an expressionist, although some aspects of her palette and brush work suggest that influence, and she is certainly never abstract expressionist, abstract, or conceptual. She was not in step with the Painters Eleven or the later work of Lawren Harris.

Salloum is not claiming that Thornton was a *great* painter. In her study of Thornton's life and art, she sets the record before her readers for them to decide what they think. She provides historical context, a list of exhibitions, many quotations from reviews of Thornton's work and from Thornton's own writing. She provides a fascinating overview of the Vancouver arts scene after the war, and she describes the challenges faced by a married woman with children who insisted on being a painter in an era when such behaviour was discouraged. Most important, she includes a broad selection of images reproduced in colour, and they provide the evidence we need to weigh Mildred Valley Thornton's contribution to the artistic history of her province and country. These pictures enable us to reconsider Thornton's work in the context of better known Canadian artists who painted native subjects and First Nations' portraits—Paul Kane, Emily Carr and Nicholas de Grandmaison.

In my view, she is an important painter and a worthy spokeswoman for her time and place. She deserves to be recognized, with her best work preserved and hung for public viewing. For every great modern artist, every Picasso, Bacon, Milne or Carr, there are hundreds of artists who play minor roles, but who are essential to the development of the art form, its appreciation with the public, and its acquisition by collectors and less wealthy art lovers. Not everyone can afford a Francis Bacon. Not everyone wants to live with such work on their walls. To appreciate art, to see it as important in our lives, to understand the vital role it plays in telling us who we are is what matters most of all. This is what an artist like Thornton gives us—a sense of who we are in our time and place—and it is a priceless gift.

In a recent interview with Salloum, retired Vancouver art teacher and historian Leonard Woods commented that Mildred Valley Thornton has never been "accorded the recognition that is her due"; he went on to say that we lack a "record of her achievement" and that "if that were done, we would recover an important painter and a record of a lot of Vancouver that has disappeared" (109–10). In this book, Sheryl Salloum has provided that record.

SHERRILL GRACE
VANCOUVER, 2011

"Sometimes the urge [to paint] was so strong it was as if someone were standing over me with a whip."[1] With those words, Mildred Valley Thornton (HON. CPA, FRSA) summed up her remarkable artistic career. Throughout her life (1890–1967), she felt compelled to record the history and beauty of her country. Born at the end of the Victorian era, Mildred grew up during a time when women stayed home, reared children and looked after their husbands and households. Artistic endeavours were considered amusements and "frowned upon" as professions. Female artists "could not achieve the public presence afforded their male counterparts."[2] Undaunted, Mildred valiantly forged her own vision. Adventurous, ambitious, confident, forthright, fun-loving, independent, poetic and socially conscious, she fulfilled her artistic aspirations: she became both a professional painter and a writer, presenting images and stories of Canada's distinctive landscapes and its First Peoples. In doing so, Mildred struggled against many adversities: "Discouragement, lack, ill health, indifference—I knew them all in full measure, but persisted because I was determined to finish the job I had set out to do."[3]

That "job," which also became an obsession, was to capture in paint the visages of the aboriginal peoples of Western Canada. Their physiological features, and the personalities and experiences reflected therein, fascinated Mildred. She was not the first Canadian artist, or the first female painter, who wanted to portray this coun-

‹ Mildred Valley Thornton
in her Vancouver studio
1771 Comox Street
circa 1944
THORNTON FAMILY
PRIVATE COLLECTION
PHOTOGRAPHER UNKNOWN

try's indigenous population. She was, however, one of the most prodigious, completing approximately three hundred portraits and numerous paintings of totem poles and scenes of traditional rituals and activities. Mildred was the only Canadian artist to document so thoroughly personages from Western Canada's First Nations, particularly elders. Locally, nationally and internationally, she became the "'lady who paints Indians.'"[4] Mildred hoped to preserve the work in a Canadian gallery or museum as a historical legacy.

Landscapes (including mountain, water, city, recreational and industrial scenes in both watercolours and oils) were Mildred's other preoccupation and a source of income comprising a treasury of vibrant images of Alberta, Saskatchewan, British Columbia (B.C.) and Ontario. She thrilled at escaping the confines of domestic life, took pleasure in depicting the topographical features of her homeland and reflected that joy and pride in her work.

When Mildred died in July 1967, she was an internationally renowned artist and a Fellow of the Royal Society of Arts. During her lifetime, she was also a noted journalist, *Vancouver Sun* art critic, book reviewer, poet and recipient of a Canadian Authors' Association Award for her book, *Indian Lives and Legends*.[5] In addition, she was known as an early innovator of the arts in Regina, Saskatchewan, and a keen and influential participant in and supporter of Vancouver's artistic and literary communities. For over thirty years, she was an energizing force in the city's cultural development. Mildred was also an untiring social activist, with a special interest in issues affecting First Nations of B.C. and Canada.

For nearly forty years, Mildred pursued her self-appointed mission of preserving images of aboriginal Canadians. In the last years of her life, while suffering from a terminal blood disorder, Mildred doggedly tried to find a home for what she called her "Collection."[6] Always a champion of First Nations, she wanted part of the proceeds to "be used for scholarships and bursaries for our B.C. Indians."[7] When, on her deathbed, Mildred realized no government agency or gallery was going to purchase and preserve her work as a historical legacy, she was so anguished that she wrote a codicil to her will stating that her First Nations portraits should either be auctioned off or destroyed. To the relief of her executors and heirs, the codicil was improperly witnessed—the work remained intact. But, unsuccessful in their attempts to interest a public institution in the collection, Mildred's sons eventually sold the paintings piecemeal.

Mildred's life ended in frustration and in the belief that her bold "PROJECT"[8] had failed. Her unpublished poem "Ad Astra" reflects Mildred's courage, fortitude and resolve.

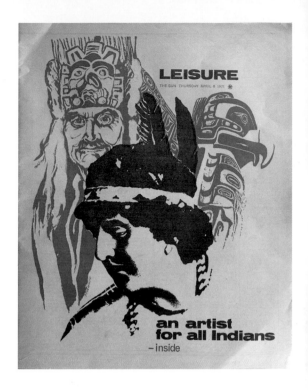

"an artist for all Indians"
Leisure, Vancouver Sun
April 8, 1971
COURTESY OF UNO
LANGMANN AND THE
VANCOUVER SUN
DAN FAIRCHILD PHOTOGRAPHY

> I would go from life as a warrior goes,
> On the striking of a blow,
> Who flings his life among his foes,
> Nor grieves to see it go.
> Or I would be quenched like a lantern hung
> To hark some difficult ledge,
> And when the need is ended, flung
> Still flaring, over the edge.
> I would leave the world as if I leapt
> To snatch a star from the sky,
> And the sky closed up its fingers and kept
> The mortal who dared too high.[9]

Sadly, after her death, the "sky" did close, obscuring Mildred's reputation. Her work and her contributions to Canadian art have been largely overlooked by art historians.[10] Yet, like the "flung" lantern, the flame of this significant artist and historical figure is "still flaring." In 1997, she was inducted as an Honorary Member of the Canadian Portrait Academy. Commercial galleries continue to exhibit and sell Mildred's paintings. First Nations people and communities value her portraits. They, and national and international collectors, are acquiring her paintings; some work is also in prominent Canadian galleries and museums.

Unlike most women of her day, Mildred "dared" to interpret and record her country in new and extraordinary ways. As feisty as she was inventive, Mildred was "forever torn between two loyalties—the inevitable fate of a married woman with both a family and a career to serve." She insisted that with "a modicum of health" there was "a way" to surmount all difficulties.[11] That "way" resulted in a lifestyle that was unorthodox for the time and an artistic production that was unique. Today, Mildred's paintings are both a historic record and a dramatic celebration of the country and peoples she so cherished. Her story, with its inspirations and struggles, is as colourful, complex and compelling as her work.

ONE

To Walk Worthily

On May 7, 1890, Mildred Valley Stinson was born on a farm a few miles from Rutherford, Ontario. Of English descent, her mother, Clara Delita Valentina Longman and nicknamed "Vally" (1863–1951), was born in Chicago. Mildred's father, Edward Stinson (1848–1929), was born in Ireland. When he was two, the Stinson family emigrated and settled in the Chatham/Dresden region of southern Ontario. Edward had four children from his first marriage and ten from his second (of which Mildred was third born). He was a "true pioneer" who became "an expert lumberman" and "one of the largest land-owning farmers in the area,"[1] raising a variety of livestock and crops such as wheat and maize.

As the responsibilities of farm women of the day included tending the livestock and the kitchen garden, Mildred likely had such chores. In her adult years, her facility with textile arts (sewing, knitting and rug hooking) would have been learned out of necessity or as preparation for her future marriage and domestic role. Perhaps the demands of such activities and the noise and bustle of life with five sisters and eight

‹ Mildred Valley Thornton
circa 1920s
PHOTO COURTESY OF
THORNTON FAMILY
PRIVATE COLLECTION
PHOTOGRAPHER UNKNOWN

1

brothers (two siblings died in childhood) developed Mildred's independence, sense of humour and her ability to empathize with and charm others. She also would have craved time alone, and reading became a cherished activity. As a result, she became fond of poetry and English literature at a young age. Her literary interests were also sparked by her mother, who had once dreamed of being a writer and kept a small library. Mildred stated that her mother's "treasured" books were

> the happy familiars of my childhood, and I can remember sitting on the floor as a small girl in the seldom-used parlour, reading Byron, Moore, Tennyson, Bryant and loving every word. I read Burns,... [George] Meredith,... Marie Corelli, George Elliot, Lord Lytton and others, but none of them interested me so much as poetry.[2]

The Pioneers, circa 1927
oil on canvas, 22" x 36"
PRIVATE COLLECTION
DAN FAIRCHILD PHOTOGRAPHY

The area around the Stinson homestead, located on the corner of the Dawn Mills Road and the Kent Line,[3] was made up of numerous communities "not much larger than a flea bite."[4] Mildred and her siblings likely attended the one-room Esterville school (Union School Section), a mile from their home.[5] School notebooks indicate that Mildred started to write poetry at a young age, and she continued to do so throughout her life. She also demonstrated an early interest in drawing and painting. Some of her inspiration may have come from her maternal grandfather, Edwin Longman, an Oxford scholar with interests in philosophy and the arts. He wrote poetry, played the organ and was an accomplished watercolour and oil painter.[6] Mildred recalled, "He used to present his children with some of his work for Christmas and… their birthdays. I suppose ours was the only house for miles around with a number of fine original paintings on the parlour walls."[7] Sometime during her younger years, Mildred began painting with watercolours and oils. In a small oil of three chicks painted during her teenage years (now owned by extended family members), her sketching ability, bold brushstrokes and competence with composition are already evident.

Mildred's childhood experiences were restricted to farm life, and that environment was the main subject available to the young artist. She later moved to Saskatchewan, strengthening her connection to her rural roots. Mildred's conception of her homeland as an important agrarian nation formed part of her artistic vision. She captured images of old farmhouses, hay fields and, occasionally, barnyard animals. Her image of pigs in a sty demonstrates Mildred's ongoing affection for and connection to Canada's agricultural heritage. She kept that painting in her personal collection, along with a small oil of ducks sauntering across a barnyard.

At the beginning of the twentieth century, life in rural Canada was "inherently patriarchal in its organization."[8] Men were the income earners, and females tended the home. Some women entered careers such as nursing and teaching, but those jobs often ended with marriage and childrearing. While Mildred's father realized "most of his children were to continue the family farming tradition," he "soon recognized

The Old Stinson Farm
(detail), n.d., watercolour
14" x 22"
PRIVATE COLLECTION
PAINTED BY EMMA JEAN ZARUNA

that Mildred's interests led elsewhere."[9] He financed her studies at Olivet College (Michigan) and the Ontario College of Art, "for which she was forever grateful."[10]

Mildred explained:

> It was a tradition that my mother's people should be educated at Olivet. Two of my uncles and an aunt—the noted sculptor, Evelyn Beatrice Longman—had preceded me.
>
> Aunt Evelyn had gone from Olivet to the Chicago Art Institute…. I was the only one in the next generation to follow in her footsteps… and people expected me to walk worthily therein.[11]

That desire "to walk worthily" seems to have weighed heavily on Mildred over the years, especially in light of her aunt's reputation. In the 1893 St. Louis Exposition, Longman won recognition for her sculpture of a male figure, *Victory*. She became the only female assistant to the noted American sculptor Daniel Chester French and helped him with his most famous commission, the Lincoln Memorial in Washington, D.C. Although public sculptures were deemed a male domain, Longman built an esteemed reputation for such work. Unlike Mildred, who supported women's causes, Longman never joined or was affiliated with women's organizations. Unfortunately, there are no records of communication or interaction between the two women, but Mildred seems to have held her aunt in high regard, keeping and even sometimes exhibiting a plaster cast of one of Longman's sculptural reliefs.

In 1919, when Mildred was twenty-nine, her aunt became the first woman given full membership in America's National Academy of Design. Mildred must have been proud of and motivated by her aunt's success. Moreover, the need to prove herself may have influ-

Pigs in the Barnyard
n. d., oil on board
8½" x 10"
PRIVATE COLLECTION
DAN FAIRCHILD PHOTOGRAPHY

enced Mildred's artistic choices. Works such as *The Pioneers* (circa 1927) and *Old Hudson's Bay Trading Post, Fort Qu'Appelle* (circa 1920) indicate that Mildred was searching for subjects with iconic qualities particular to Canada. Bison, a major source of food and mythology for the ancestral prairie First Nations and an enduring symbol of the North American Plains after European con-

tact, became one such motif. Eventually, Mildred's fondness for the colourful First Nations art, crafts, customs and regalia she viewed over the years (the Lenape during her childhood and the various prairie peoples when she lived in Saskatchewan) inspired her lifelong passion for painting aboriginal peoples and events.

A vivacious brunette with steel-blue eyes, Mildred Stinson was just seventeen when she enrolled at Olivet College in 1907 and the only Canadian in both her freshman and sophomore classes.[12] She must have been excited at experiencing a different country, landscape and new ideas; however, she remained "violently patriotic" and draped a Union Jack over the head of her bed.[13] Like many young people leaving home for the first time, Mildred suffered over her separation from family, especially such a large and apparently close-knit group of siblings. In a poem titled "On Homesickness," she wrote

> The night fell slowly and dreary
> And my heart was rent with pain
> ....
> I longed for the dear home faces....[14]

Mildred grew up in a society that stressed family, hard work and independence. There was "a Victorian Protestant culture in Ontario that emphasized the relationship between social stability and Protestant morality.... The moral code was strict, but chiefly voluntary and individualistic."[15] As an adult, Mildred was never a regular churchgoer; however, she adhered to her uncompromising ethical principles.

Olivet College, a coeducational Christian facility, seems to have shaped Mildred's values while reinforcing her Protestant upbringing. Founded by Reverend John J. Shipherd in 1844, the College supported abolition and an education that was open to all regardless of gender, race or social status. The student body was also taught the importance of community service. Today, Olivet College's mission statement reflects its early commitment to provide "an education which will enrich lives intellectually, morally and spiritually… [and] our hope is that our graduates will embody the Divine art and science of doing good to others as stated by the founding fathers of Olivet."[16] Such ideals must have resonated with Mildred. After embarking on her career, she dedicated herself to developing and supporting art communities; and she became an advocate for women's causes, racial minorities and those who she felt were receiving unfair treatment.

In 1910, Mildred had completed her "Normal Art Course." According to the College catalogues, her classes included "Drawing, Perspective, Water Color, Design, Methods, and Composition." She earned an art supervisor's certificate that qualified graduates to work in private or public schools. Mildred "stubbornly" turned down offers to teach in the U.S. because she was "eager… to teach in Canada, but no position… was available." Mildred lived in Toronto for a few years and said she "briefly"[17] attended the Ontario College of Art.[18] There she studied under George A. Reid (1860–1947) and John William Beatty (1869–1941), major figures in Canadian art education. Mildred's interests in painting historical Canadian subjects may have been encouraged by both instructors. In 1899, Reid decorated Toronto's City Hall with images of Ontario settlers. Early in Beatty's career, he declared his intention to paint murals depicting Canada's history, but the studies were never undertaken.

The effect of Reid's instruction on Mildred's work is less obvious than that of Beatty. The specific classes she took from Beatty are not known, but Mildred attended one of his three-month summer school sessions at Port Hope, Ontario.[19] Besides being a noted art instructor, he was a strong patriot. Canadian nationalism was surging during the early years of the twentieth century and, like many other Toronto artists, he rejected European-like pastoral scenes. A forerunner of the Group of Seven, Beatty was among the first artists to venture to Ontario's north for inspiration. He knew several members of the Group of Seven, sketched with J.E.H. MacDonald and seems to have influenced Tom Thomson's early work: in several 1912–1913 paintings, Thomson employed Beatty's compositional style and "the same low horizon and subdued colours."[20] While Thomson and the Group of Seven undertook fresh perspectives, Beatty's work remained more atmospheric and his palette less robust.

Beatty's landscapes, precise compositions filled with light and rhythm, reflected a

mix of impressionism and realism. He was known to produce quick outdoor sketches of "visual liveliness" that were later worked up into larger canvasses (a method that Mildred also commonly used). Recurring among his motifs were trees and stumps mottled with light and shade; when she moved to B.C., such thematic elements became preferred subjects for Mildred. An "impressionistic breakup" of colourful skies, also employed by Beatty, may have inspired Mildred's dramatic cloud formations. Much of her early work on the prairies reflected his preference for low horizons. Furthermore, Beatty favoured "touches of limegreen [sic] and orange" in his palette,[21] and those colours are sometimes found in Mildred's early canvasses. One obviously early but undated and untitled Thornton painting, now called *Prairie Landscape*, is reminiscent of Beatty in its compositional technique and use of light and colour.[22]

Most artists come under various influences as they seek to develop their own unique methods and interpretations. According to Mildred's son, Jack, one of her

Toronto Cityscape, n. d.
oil on board, 10" x 13½"
PRIVATE COLLECTION
DAN FAIRCHILD PHOTOGRAPHY

Prairie Landscape, n. d.
oil on canvas, 18" x 24"
PRIVATE COLLECTION
DAN FAIRCHILD PHOTOGRAPHY

mantras was that one must never copy.[23] She absorbed Beatty's instruction and then developed her own style. In 1932, Mildred reacted sharply to the accusation in an unidentified article[24] that Beatty's influence was reflected in her portrait of Senator Arthur Meighen (former Conservative Party leader and Canada's ninth prime minister). In her defense, Mildred wrote:

> Any success I may have achieved has been won at the cost of years of constant and untiring personal effort and I strongly resent the inference…. It is my own individual and original interpretation of my subject and was executed apart from the influence of anyone whomsoever.[25]

Although Beatty was a forceful individual with a "violent and uninhibited"[26] vocabulary, Mildred nonetheless respected his artistic style and patriotism. Also like

Beatty, she admired Tom Thomson, with whom Beatty painted in Algonquin Park. After Thomson drowned in Canoe Lake in 1917, Beatty supervised the erection of a memorial cairn in the park. Possibly due to Beatty's influence, Thomson appears to have been one of Mildred's favourite artists. In her unpublished writings, there is both a poem and an article glorifying Thomson's character and work.

Over the years, as he viewed "the work of some promising students," such as George Pepper, Yvonne McKague Houser and Kathleen Daly Pepper, Beatty hoped one or more "might develop into a distinctively Canadian artist."[27] He may have felt that Mildred had fulfilled that role as the two remained in contact over the years. While stopping in Regina in the early 1930s to lecture to the Women's Canadian Club on "The Past, Present and Future of Art in Canada," Beatty stayed a night or two with Mildred and her husband.[28] After her death, Anthony Westbridge, of Westbridge Fine Art in Vancouver, identified a Beatty canvas amongst Mildred's paintings, demonstrating her lasting affection for the man and his work.

After Mildred completed her studies at the Ontario College of Art, a fascination with new panoramas and a yearning for adventure took the twenty-three-year-old from southern Ontario to Saskatchewan: "With little more than her paint box she traveled alone in a 'colonist car' of the Grand Trunk Pacific Railway as far as Regina."[29] She said she took this trip because

> everybody was talking about the West, so I decided to go and see for myself what it was like. I bought an excursion ticket to Moose Jaw, visited my uncle at Briercrest for a couple of months, and had such a good time (the Irish) that I lost the return end of my ticket and had to stay, willy nilly, because I wouldn't let the folks back home know I had been so careless (the proud English). I never did find it.[30]

Mildred never elucidated what the "good time" was. She likely enjoyed the freedom from studies and responsibilities. Perhaps she also partook of alcohol and blamed the resulting partying for the embarrassing loss of her ticket. This is only speculation, but at some point, Mildred became a teetotaler and remained one for the duration of her life. She may also have been emulating her father who, while adept at cursing, did not smoke, drink or gamble. Additionally, she may have been reflecting the ideas of the Women's Christian Temperance Movement, which originated in Picton, Ontario, and "spread rapidly across Canada in the 1880s."[31] Mildred's escapade did leave one lasting impression on the young artist. On a railway station platform, she viewed "a be-robed

Indian of such noble countenance that she at once decided that here was the subject for her brush and Regina was where she would settle."[32]

From the time she was a small girl, Mildred had observed the Lenape people from the Delaware Nation. There was little in the rolling farmland of southern Ontario to spark the imagination of a creative youngster. The Lenape stood out. Mildred's

> first memories of Indians were of those who came in the summertime, whole wagonloads of them, to sell their fine baskets.... They had good baskets, better than those the stores sold and much more colorful; skillfully contrived they were and in many beautiful shapes. Like the country stores, if you didn't have ready cash, the Indians would take in exchange butter, eggs, or anything they needed.... They fascinated me and when they went over the hill in their creaking wagons and happy carefree manner, a bit of my heart always went with them.[33]

Perhaps because she was busy starting her career, Mildred did not begin painting First Nations people until 1928. After settling in Regina in 1913, she made a living giving private painting lessons and selling landscape and portrait studies. She later became an instructor at Regina College, where, for a time, she was head of the art department.[34] The Regina College School of Art became one of Canada's important creative centres,[35] beginning with the arrival of British landscape artists Inglis Sheldon-Williams (1870–1940), James Henderson (1871–1951) and, later, Augustus Kenderdine (1870–1947). "Their paintings tended to reflect... the powerful effect of the dominant sky and its spectacular flood of light,"[36] observes author Ken Mitchell. Mildred's vibrant palette and aggressive brushstrokes set her apart, although her subject matter was primarily pastoral. She not only captured haystacks, wooden grain elevators and farmer's houses and fields, she also depicted lakes, towns, buildings and human activities such as boating and sunbathing. Mildred's paintings from the 1920s and 1930s were described by her contemporaries in Regina as having "remarkable power and fidelity."[37]

Sometime after settling in Regina, the outgoing young painter met and fell in love with the reserved John Henry Thornton (1885–1958). Nearly a year after the start of World War I, they married on April 28, 1915. Little is known of John's family, other than they were in the British steel business. A file cutting mechanic from Sheffield, England, at a young age, he joined the Mercantile Marine. His Certificate of Discharge, issued in 1911 in Sydney, Australia, listed him as an "Assistant Baker." No

one knows how or why John journeyed to Saskatchewan, but he first lived in Moose Jaw (1909) and joined a church choir. John then moved to Regina. For a few years, he worked as a payroll clerk for the nearby provincially operated "man-made islands on Wascana Lake."[38] Quiet and industrious, he proved himself a capable businessperson, operating an establishment called Andrew's "J.H. Thornton, Prop." (specializing in cakes and pastries). He also became a partner in Fell's Confectionery, a business that was eventually renamed Thornton & Benson Refreshment Parlour. According to Mildred's son, Jack, that restaurant was "a grand edifice… [with] seating capacity for at least fifty people."[39]

Jack recalls his father's enjoyments were his membership in the Masonic Order (Assiniboia Lodge No. 49 and Victoria Lodge No. 59) and Knights Templar (Wascana Preceptory). John also occasionally performed in amateur musical productions and was a member of the New Chanters male choir (Wa Wa Temple). Jack remembers that his father's staff put on a pantomime every Christmas, and John "liked to play the leading role." As became evident over the years, John's overriding interest was supporting his wife's artistic career. John was a Victorian gentleman who never left the house without wearing a tie—later in life, a bow tie. Jack says he cannot remember his father without a full suit, a white collar and a watch chain. Those who knew him describe John as always gentle and in the background. In contrast, Mildred was energetic and animated. In an unpublished writing, she noted the positive aspects of husbands who were "dependable like the old oak table." She stressed that a husband did not require "the heady wine of excessive imagination for connubial happiness." Instead, John provided "whatever of opportunity lieth in his power and a boundless enthusiasm." As different as they were, John obviously enjoyed Mildred's adventurous spirit, and she definitely appreciated his unwavering support.

Just prior to the end of the Great War, and in the third year of marriage, Mildred enrolled at the Art Institute of Chicago. In 1913, the school had startled the city by

Boat on Wascana Lake
n. d., oil on board
7" x 9⅝"
PRIVATE COLLECTION
DAN FAIRCHILD PHOTOGRAPHY

In Wascana Park, n. d.
oil on cardboard
8" x 10"
PRIVATE COLLECTION
WESTBRIDGE PHOTO

hosting the famous Armory Show, a sprawling exhibition of avant-garde European painting and sculpture. Nothing is known of her time in Chicago, but Mildred's registration records indicate that she took classes for two semesters (1918–1919).[40] John seems to have stayed home and worked while Mildred pursued her interests.

Once back in Regina, Mildred immersed herself in the developing cultural community of the new province's capital city. She became a member of the Local Council of Women, the Regina Sketch Club and the Saskatchewan Women's Art Association. She helped found the Saskatchewan Painters' Guild and was a member of the Poetry Group, a branch of the Canadian Authors' Association. She chaired the Group in 1934 and was cited as deserving "all credit for the recent successful provincial competition... [the first undertaken by that branch of the Canadian Authors' Association] and for the publication of the first poetry year book."[41] Mildred further busied herself organizing poetry readings and conferences and helped to develop the artistic and literary talents of local individuals and initiatives. She also gave lectures on art. For instance, in 1929, she spoke to the Women's Art Association on "Art Appreciation," stressing that Canadian art had to be judged on its own standards. She explained that the country's artists were depicting the beauty of its unique landscape. She also "put in a plea" for Canadian artists, stating many were "in need of sympathy and encouragement, in the work they... do,... which may some day bring honor to the Dominion."[42]

In the early years of the twentieth century, Ken Mitchell notes that the very few Saskatchewan art exhibitions "were associated with agricultural exhibitions and fairs—even rodeos and horse sales."[43] Having a scarcity of local venues to showcase or sell her work, Mrs. J.H. Thornton, as she was then known, held showings in her home, and a solo exhibition (1921 or 1922) was sponsored by the Local Council of Women.[44] In 1930, she exhibited over fifty paintings (landscapes and portraits) in the grand Canadian Pacific Railway lodging, Hotel Saskatchewan. James F. Bryant, a provincial cabinet minister, "paid tribute to her as one of Saskatchewan's most outstanding artists." He also noted that she "was the first Saskatchewan artist to give an exhibition of her own paintings."[45]

Mildred's reputation brought some eminent sitters to her studio. Professionals such as doctors and writers, and members of provincial and federal political parties, were always part of Mildred's social circle. At differing times during her career, she seems to have contemplated a specialization in portraits of important political figures.[46] Circa 1930, she completed a portrait of C.D. Cowan, Saskatchewan Conservative Member of Parliament and former Regina mayor. On June 21, 1934, Cowan wrote from Ottawa to tell Mildred that he would soon be returning to Regina, and on his "programme" was a visit. He signed off by telling her, "Now get your philosophy ready,"[47] indicating that, as a member of the Regina Debating Club, he enjoyed discussions with the Thorntons. Like John, Cowan was a Mason; like Mildred, he supported temperance. Cowan's portrait now hangs on the main floor of Regina's City Hall.

In 1932, Mildred's portrait of Arthur Meighen was described as being "full of strength and character. There is tremendous expression in the eyes…. Simple and broad in treatment, decisive in color and excellent as to likeness, it is a picture of dignity and power."[48] The portrait was donated to the Arthur Meighen Club of Regina, but the painting's whereabouts is currently unknown.

Mildred's study of Sir Frederick Haultain (circa 1933), the first premier of the Northwest Territories and a chancellor of the University of Saskatchewan, was described thus: "A kindly quizzical expression kindles his features. The pose is easy and graceful, and the picture has distinction and charm."[49] Haultain's portrait is now in the archives of the Fort, Museum of the North-West Mounted Police in Fort Macleod.

Distinctions continued to come Mildred's way. After exhibiting at the Canadian National Exhibition (1931 and 1932) in Toronto, her portraits of Haultain and Meighen were accepted in two esteemed 1933 juried exhibitions: the Ontario Society of Artists (OSA) and the Montreal Museum of Fine Arts. Furthermore, Mildred was "the first resident Saskatchewan artist to be represented in… these organizations, [and] it is believed that this constitutes a record in Saskatchewan art." As well, her oil *Prairie Town (near Punnichy)* was lauded for its "broad sweeping strokes"[50] when shown at the 1933 OSA exhibition. Although she was never a member (nor was

Tilly Jean Rolston, circa 1950s, oil on canvas 32" x 26"
IMAGE PDP02813
COURTESY OF ROYAL BC MUSEUM, BC ARCHIVES

Sunlight and Shadows
n.d., oil on board
8½" x 10½"
PRIVATE COLLECTION
DAN FAIRCHILD PHOTOGRAPHY

British Columbian painter Emily Carr, 1871–1945), Mildred's *In the Touchwood Hills, Saskatchewan* was accepted for the 1932 exhibition of the Royal Canadian Academy of Arts (RCA).[51] This organization was founded in 1880, with one of its objectives being the establishment of a national art gallery. In 1934, Mildred had two prairie landscapes exhibited by the RCA: *Foreclosed* and *Bulwarks of the Prairie*. Amongst the other work shown that year was Frederick Varley's *Dhârâna*. In 1941, Mildred's portrait *Dominic Jack, Okanagan Indian* was accepted.[52]

Because she was deemed among the province's most eminent artists, Mildred was asked to assemble a collection of oil and watercolour paintings to represent Saskatchewan art and artists at the 1930 Canadian National Exhibition (CNE). For the first time, only Canadian work (historical and contemporary) was being featured. B.C. exhibitors included Emily Carr, T.W. Fripp, Harry Hood, Frederick Varley, Ina D. Uhthoff and W.P. Weston. Mildred showed a watercolour, *Dutch Girl*.[53] She stated that an all-Canadian exhibition was "in keeping with the remarkable strides Canada was making towards achieving a national art" and was a "show-window" for the country's "progress as a nation." Echoing John William Beatty and other nationalists, she stressed,

> Too often in art distance lends enchantment and to say that a picture was European sometimes invested it with a glamor that far exceeded its real value while the genius of our own country was left to languish in obscurity. Today people are beginning to realize that only insofar as art is a physical and spiritual interpretation of the nation can it be termed great. That Canada has many painters whose work possesses these qualities none can deny.[54]

Mildred further extolled that, for those attending the CNE, the art exhibition was a place to "enter into quiet communion with the aesthetic elements that exalt and elevate the race."[55] Five years later, in 1935, the innovative West Coast photographer John Vanderpant, who later became a friend of Mildred's, expressed the same idea: "Genuine art must emotionally and by analyses exalt and elevate."[56] That idea was in keeping with the mystical beliefs held by many artists of the day and reflected the idea that art was an essential and guiding component of life. In another address, Mildred identified what she felt were the qualities necessary if an artist was to successfully convey aesthetic interpretations: "Courage, daring and a vigorous mentality"[57]—qualities she exhibited throughout her life.

TWO

An Artist Through and Through

In March 1926, during the first trimester of her pregnancy with twin sons, Jack and Maitland, Mildred journeyed to Algonquin Park, Ontario, with a number of other artists for two weeks of camping and painting. Although John William Beatty had surgery sometime in 1926, he may have organized this trip and been a participant. The Algonquin trip, like other painting expeditions she took in later years, was difficult and uncomfortable. Mildred noted that the journey, through "five feet of snow" and a temperature of twenty-five degrees below zero (F), to Mowat Lodge on Canoe Lake was "a five mile ride with a fair-sized straw stack beneath us in the big sleigh box, and layers of heavy blankets." She did not seem to mind, however, because finding herself in Tom Thomson's locale "was like stepping into the sacred precincts of mystical territory." A watercolour painting of the storm-tossed waters where Thomson lost his life illustrates "the lonely shores"[1] of the lake. Some of Mildred's inspiration and

‹ *Grain Elevator and Railway Tracks*, n.d.
oil on canvas, 24" x 30"
PRIVATE COLLECTION
DAN FAIRCHILD PHOTOGRAPHY

Canoe Lake, Algonquin Park
1926, watercolour, 6¾" X 9¼"
PRIVATE COLLECTION
DAN FAIRCHILD PHOTOGRAPHY

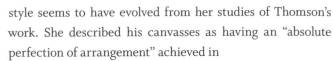

Photograph of Mildred with Jack
(right) and Maitland, circa 1936
VANDERPANT GALLERIES
THORNTON FAMILY
PRIVATE COLLECTION

style seems to have evolved from her studies of Thomson's work. She described his canvasses as having an "absolute perfection of arrangement" achieved in

> a thorough workman-like manner, painting every inch of his canvas with careful deliberation, and confident understanding of his subject…. All he had to do was be true to his own inner reactions… keen perception and unerring precision. He laid his colors on in clear bars of prismatic purity. His analysis of tone was penetrating and true. There is an elemental grandeur and a bold simplicity about his work which faithfully depicts the Canadian scene.[2]

In both her landscape and portrait work, Mildred also preferred to use colours of "prismatic purity." Like Thomson, Mildred demonstrated strong draftsmanship and confidence and was guided by her "keen perception." She also sought to create distinctive Canadian images that were both simple and striking.

On October 9, 1926, Mildred gave birth to John Milton (nicknamed "Jack") and Walter Maitland (who preferred his middle name). For a woman whose life centered on painting, becoming a mother at thirty-six must have been overwhelming. She

could not have found much time away from the demands of two infants. As soon as they were old enough for such outings, she took her sons with her on painting trips; in later childhood, the twins chose to stay home with their father. Forays away from her husband and boys were not well looked upon by Mildred's relatives or the general public. Some family members and her older sister Ida Stinson Webster, in particular, believed "it was fine for… [Mildred] to paint, but thought she should be home with her kids."[3]

During the early part of the twentieth century, painting was viewed as mainly a male profession. Female artists were often considered dilettantes or hobbyists. Women's lives were supposed to revolve around family and home, and those who behaved or chose otherwise were thought to be eccentric (like Emily Carr) or neglectful wives and mothers. But as Lara T. Evoy, Mildred's great-great-niece, has indicated in her art history thesis on Mildred, this did not mean women were "passive or indifferent observers in their own lives. [Rather,] women have continuously (re)negotiated their positions; publicly, through their work, their art and social activism, as well as privately, in their own families and personal relationships."[4] Mildred often tried to negate criticism of her absences by explaining the rigorous preparations she undertook prior to a trip: "I would bake for days and load up the fridge with food so that John would have as little cooking to do as possible during my absence."[5]

Mildred never seems to have doubted her calling or her abilities. She was luckier than most other Canadian female artists of the era in that she had a husband who understood, encouraged and financially supported her endeavours. John allowed Mildred the freedom she needed, even when he had to assume the care of the household and children for months at a time. Jack says his mother

was certainly not a cook or a housekeeper. She spent most of her time in her studio, painting, or going away on trips; my father really raised my brother and me. My dad did most of the cooking. We grew up thinking that you ate bacon and eggs three times a day. When I joined the navy and was in basic training on the ships everyone else said, "The food's terrible!" I thought it was bloody good compared to what I had been used to.

In spite of Mildred's busy schedule and domestic shortcomings, Jack insists that he and Maitland never suffered. They grew accustomed to their mother's absences and found her supportive and encouraging when she was home. Mildred tended them without complaint through the childhood diseases of the day: chickenpox, measles, mumps and whooping cough. She also nursed them through bouts of flu and Maitland's 1932 pneumonia. In turn, they doted on their mom. In an unpublished writing, "Reflections on 'Flu,'" Mildred gives amusing insights into life with her young boys.

One of the dearest things about my particular attack of flu was the untiring solicitude of my nine-year-old twins, vieing [sic] with each other in their efforts to serve me. I was able to listen to the crashing of dishes, the splashing of water on the kitchen floor, smell the acrid odor of burnt toast, hear the banging of the screen door with almost angelic equilibrium, for every sound was a love token. Was it not all for love of me, and no star ever shone with more brilliance in the firmament than their eyes as they proudly bore the breakfast in to my room. A pot of steaming tea—good tea too, little fingers of golden toast as dainty as you please, all properly set out on a tray. Who says boys haven't taste?... And the yearning tenderness in their clumsy little ways as they would adjust the blinds, straighten the quilts or produce a hot water bottle, longing to kiss and embrace me but restraining the desire as best they could before my admonitions... [so] that they might not contract the malady.

Prairie Storm, circa 1931
oil on board, 7" x 9¼"
MacLEAN FAMILY
PRIVATE COLLECTION
PIPPIN LEE PHOTOGRAPHY

Whether Mildred left home for more than one extended painting trip prior to having children is not clear (only one of her later journals has survived).[6] She did not drive, but she did journey out on day trips, alone or with others, to paint prairie landscapes. She often exhibited those works in her Regina home studios (they lived in several houses) because there were few other venues available. At an exhibition of Mildred's work in May 1931, she met and befriended the Reverend Duncan A. MacLean, a United Church minister. A painter himself, MacLean "found her a wonderful person."[7] A few weeks later, he stopped at Mildred's house and "had the time of my life among her paintings. I love her work. There is nothing I would rather do than use a brush like she does."[8] At the time of their meeting, MacLean was the father of three girls, including twins. (Two more daughters and a son would follow.) He and his family lived in Wilcox and later, Raymore, Saskatchewan (two towns near Regina); he ministered to congregations in these communities, as well as to those in three other nearby settlements. MacLean had little time to pursue his painting, but did so as often as possible. He also called on the Thorntons whenever he could. He sometimes brought them eggs and on a few occasions stayed for tea or dinner, or as an overnight guest. An accomplished carpenter, MacLean made Mildred stretchers, an easel, a paint box and a small table. As recorded in MacLean's diaries, at least once, on February 16, 1932, he matted and framed one of Mildred's watercolours. On October 7, 1931, he and Mildred went on their first sketching trip together.

As well as being the parents of twins, the two artists were kindred spirits, sharing a passion for the prairie landscape and an interest in helping the exploited or under-privileged. MacLean's daughter, Katheryn (Kae) MacLean Broughton, describes her father as "a social democrat like Tommy Douglas. The fact that people weren't treated fairly hurt him. He would do or say things to try to implement social reforms, and he was always in trouble. People called him a communist."[9] His friendship with Mildred sheds light on her career, personality and family life. She and MacLean shared the difficulty of finding time to paint and enjoyed several painting trips together. His diary entry of March 14, 1932 indicates that, in spite of roads which were "very bad," they "went to Hungry Hollow... to get a snow sketch or two." On another outing (September 15, 1932), they drove to a lake north of Punnichy, not arriving until 4:00 PM. MacLean only had time to make one sketch before losing the light. How many Mildred made is unknown but, never one to miss an opportunity, she captured the sunset as they drove home.

In 1933, they only managed a few outings, and on September 5, 1933, MacLean lamented, "I have tried over and over to get the use of a car for the day but I cannot get one.... I want to take Mrs. Thornton to some historic spots in the hills country for sketching purposes and I am balked." Alone, or with someone else, Mildred did make an earlier trip to that part of the country. Her canvas, *The Touchwood Hills* (circa 1930), is in the National Gallery of Canada.

The proximity of the two painters on their sketching trips in the country might suggest that romantic feelings had developed between them. Canada's most artistic preacher, the fictional Philip Bentley in Sinclair Ross's *As for Me and My House,* was seemingly tormented by such feelings. But there is no evidence in MacLean's diaries or accounts of Mildred's life that this was the case. She had a supportive, loving husband and two sons she prized. What MacLean provided Mildred was something more important than a romantic escapade—that is, an opportunity to pursue her obsession to paint. As for MacLean, he obviously cherished the time with and the encouragement of a sophisticated artist.

Margaret MacLean recalls her father returning home after a painting excursion with Mildred. He told the family that, while the two were working on their landscapes, a storm suddenly developed. Determined to complete her painting, Mildred "attacked the canvas," throwing the paint on as she captured the scene, including "the threatening black clouds." That painting later hung in the MacLean manse, and his youngest daughter, Oriole, "was always frightened" by the powerful image.[10]

Kae Broughton notes that her father was a talented painter: "He undertook graduate work in New York City in both arts and theology."[11] In his diaries, MacLean noted that Mildred worked quickly, often completing two sketches to his one. Speed was a characteristic of Mildred's work and life, since she had to juggle her domestic duties and childcare with her artistic pursuits. Mildred was quick to judge what a painting needed, and MacLean sometimes "learned from Mildred. One time they were painting the same scene together, and she reached over with her paintbrush and put in a couple of flakes of red. Dad was just floored because the red made the painting."[12]

Soon after meeting MacLean, Mildred asked if she could paint his portrait. She posed him with his eyes looking outward and away from the viewer. He seems to be lost in a contemplation that could be philosophical, spiritual or creative. The size of his hands (which along with the face is considered to reflect the soul of the portrait subject) suggests they hold special powers to guide, heal or construct.

Kae recalls that, unbeknownst to Mildred, the portrait caused her father some discomfort. As he wrote in his diary (November 11, 1931), "I feel a little silly in doing this and yet I am getting a great kick out of it." He also noted that, in that first sitting, "she made rapid progress." He posed six more times, once for two hours. Mildred exhibited the portrait, and a journalist described the painting as having "a serious dignity."[13] After exhibiting the work, she gave MacLean the portrait. He did not mention his reaction to the finished work in his diary. Kae notes that the painting was "huge." She feels her dad was both "embarrassed and flattered by it. As a clergyman, he found it very egotistical to hang a painting of himself in the house. He didn't know what to do with it." Mildred

often visited, and she would be hurt if the painting were not on view, "so it had to be hung." MacLean picked what he thought to be the most inconspicuous spot: the top of the stairs. Kae laughs,

> If you looked in the window of the front door, there he was at the top of the stairs. One little girl told us she came to the door and knocked and knocked: "Mr. MacLean was at the top of the stairs, and he wouldn't answer!"[14]

The family never told Mildred that story, but, a jovial person, she would undoubtedly have chuckled.

Kae recalls that Mildred "was quite pretty," with brown hair tinged with red and worn in ringlets. Kae further remembers that Mildred could be

~ Jack and Maitland Thornton circa 1930s, THORNTON FAMILY PRIVATE COLLECTION PHOTO BY MILDRED VALLEY THORNTON

> quite gruff. She took on the task of washing our hands and faces before and after meals. She was so thorough and so rough that we wondered if we would have any skin left when she was finished! I think Mrs. Thornton decided that was one thing she could do, as she might have felt some guilt: after all, she was freeloading a bit. Mother was left to supervise all the children and make all the meals while Dad and Mrs. Thornton went off to paint from nature.[15]

Kae and her twin sister, Rae, were a day older than Jack and Maitland. They played with the boys when they were between the ages of five and eight. The girls found it "fun" to have another set of twins for playmates. Kae found Miltie and Maitie, as they were called, "delightful. They could draw anything, and they would challenge one another to drawing contests."[16] According to Jack, Mildred never taught her boys to draw. Their talent was natural, and Mildred always offered encouragement.

On October 9, 1931, MacLean took his twins and their sister Margaret to Jack and Maitland's fifth birthday party. In his diary, he wrote, "Had a big time." Kae concurs, adding that, even as a youngster, she found that Mildred's "strength of character… and enthusiasm" was impressive. "She really cared for her family and was most likely torn between her domestic responsibilities and her painting. I think that must have been hard for her. She was an artist through and through."[17]

THREE

A Very Enthusiastic Woman

Life changed dramatically for the Thorntons during the 1930s. Where John had once been prosperous, the Depression ruined his restaurant business. On August 16, 1934, John left Regina for Vancouver. Shortly after, Mildred and the boys followed, making their way west by train. Her departure was described as "a distinct loss to Saskatchewan."[1] Jack remembers that for a brief time the family lived in a boarding house (10th Avenue and Alberta Street):

> We had one room with two beds for the four of us—no other furniture. We shared a kitchen with several Eastern European families, none of whom spoke English. There was no Christmas tree, let alone anything to put under it. Things were pretty tough.

Jack wonders how the more than one hundred of his mother's paintings were moved to B.C., where they were stored during the latter years of the Depression, and how she managed money for paint and other supplies. Whether it was John's idea

‹ *Coal Harbour,* n.d.
oil on board, 9½" x 13½"
THORNTON FAMILY
PRIVATE COLLECTION
PHOTO BY JANET DWYER

or Mildred's, she and her eight-year-old twins soon left Vancouver for Toronto. Where John stayed is unknown—possibly the same boarding house. Alone and friendless in a new city, he must have suffered many apprehensions. Mildred and the boys would have been anxious, but for seven months, they lived more comfortably than in their cramped Vancouver quarters. They stayed with an art school chum of Mildred's, Alice Innes. A single woman, she lived in a small apartment on North Young Street. Jack recalls that Canadian Senator Arthur Meighen sometimes visited. He once gave each twin a fifty-cent piece—a heady sum for a child in those days. Jack does not remember Mildred painting in the close confines; however, a newspaper article recounts that, while in Toronto, Mildred sold "a considerable amount of her work, including illustrations."[2] Whether Mildred sold paintings she had moved across the country or work undertaken in Toronto is unknown; whether she sent the money to John or used it to pay for room and board is also unclear.

Meanwhile, in Vancouver, John managed to open a small confectionery store near the corner of Main Street and Broadway. Next, he rented a house (3rd Avenue and Alma Street), and Mildred and the boys returned to Vancouver via the Canadian Pacific Railway. En route, she made numerous lightning-quick watercolour sketches of the passing scenery. A year later, the family took up residence at 405 West 13th Avenue. Jack says Mildred often helped in the Broadway sweets shop, which he thinks may have been called Honeydew Confectionery. Jack does not remember his mother painting much during that time, which was likely disheartening and stressful for her.

According to Jack, street parties were sometimes held on Main Street in an attempt to assuage the hardships of the citizenry: "People moved up and down Main Street listening to music and dancing. The candy store did well during those parties." Afterwards, trying to earn a little extra for the family, the twins pulled a wagon along the street collecting bottles. One time Jack and Maitland only "got half of what the bottles were worth. Father really scolded us for not getting the exact amount. It might only have been a few cents, and it seems silly now, but every penny was important at that time." Before long, John closed the confectionery and found full-time work as a baker. He later managed the Polly Ann Bakeries, a division of Safeway. Jack does not recall his father baking at home or ever bringing home baked goods. As well, even though John had managed restaurants, he did not cook much beyond simple fare and only did that when Mildred was away. When home, cleaning and cooking were her domain—a reflection of the upbringings of Mildred and John and the social mores of the day.

As soon as she and the twins returned to Vancouver, Mildred immediately involved herself with the city's artistic and cultural communities. In May 1935, she announced her presence with an exhibition at the Hudson's Bay store. On the fifth floor, customers and art aficionados viewed aboriginal portraits of "arresting interest,"[3] studies Mildred had been painting since 1928. She also displayed *The Rider of the Plains* (circa 1930), a heroic depiction of a lone officer patrolling a vast prairie expanse. A watercolour rendition of that painting was reproduced on the 1937 covers of the Canadian Pacific Railway dining car menus under the title *The Mountie*.[4] In keeping with her historical interests, Mildred also showed a rendering of the Regina North-West Mounted Police barracks where Louis Riel had awaited execution. Over the years, Mildred taught private sketching and watercolour classes, some in her Vancouver home and some at the Commercial and Fine Arts Training Centre.

The Rider of the Plains
n. d., oil on canvas
measurements unknown
REPRODUCED FROM KODACHROME
SLIDE IN THORNTON FAMILY
PRIVATE COLLECTION, DIGITALLY
RESTORED BY JANET DWYER

By August 1936, Mildred was busy preparing for a solo exhibition at the Vancouver Art Gallery. Eighty-eight works were hung. She continued to show her art in solo exhibitions such as the one held in 1942 at B.C.'s Provincial Museum. From 1935 to 1950, she often exhibited with the Annual B.C. Artists Exhibition. Her work also hung in many of the B.C. Society of Fine Arts (BCFSA) annual exhibitions from 1942 to 1959 (in 1950, the name was changed to the B.C. Society of Artists). In such exhibitions, her images hung with that of other notable B.C. artists: for example, in the BCFSA 1942 exhibition, her paintings were displayed with work by B.C. Binning, Emily Carr, Lilias Farley, Lawren Harris, Irene Hoffar-Reid, Maud Sherman and W.P. Weston.

Life slowly improved for the Thorntons. In 1939, after inhabiting a few other residences, the family bought a large, old three-storey frame house at 1771 Comox Street, near English Bay. The bedrooms were on the top floor; the kitchen, living room and dining room were on the main level. Mildred liked the large light-filled dining area and took that space over as her studio. Jack recounts that he and Maitland would be heading off to school and Mildred would already be at work, standing before her

Boats at Kitsilano, n. d.
pen-and-ink sketch
8½" x 13"
PRIVATE COLLECTION
DAN FAIRCHILD PHOTOGRAPHY

easel and wielding her brushes. In search of inspiration for her landscape work, Mildred traveled by train, trolley, bus, friends' cars or on foot to such nearby places as Burrard Inlet, Kitsilano Beach, Stanley Park and the University of British Columbia, to Vancouver's suburbs and up the coast to areas like Squamish. She also journeyed throughout numerous areas of B.C. (including the Cariboo, the Kootenays and the Okanagan), painting aboriginal peoples' portraits and the varying topography.

The 1940s were Mildred's most productive years in terms of her artistic and cultural endeavours and her social advocacy. She had affiliations with at least ten organizations, often becoming an executive member. One such group was the Soroptimist Club, a charitable international women's organization that aims "to provide educational funding for the advancement of human rights and the status of women."[5] Another philanthropic group with which Mildred was connected was the Imperial Order of Daughters of the Empire (IODE). During the war years, Mildred—whose sons were then in the navy—encouraged other artists to portray "the tremendous and eventful days"[6] of the conflict and to support the war effort. She wrote articles and reviews encouraging art auctions in support of the Red Cross. In 1943, she held a solo exhibition at the Vancouver YMCA to aid the St. Mary's Spitfire Fund.

Mildred was an executive member of the Community Arts Council in 1947/1948 and 1949/1950. Among the Council's cultural endeavours was the ambitious 1949 exhibit at the Vancouver Art Gallery (VAG), Design For Living, that 14,000 people attended.[7] Mildred also became actively involved with the Canadian Authors' Association, eventually serving as president of the Vancouver branch and national vice-president for B.C. and Alberta. Frank Wade, a former president of the Vancouver branch, recalls that Mildred

> was a very enthusiastic woman. From time to time, she lectured to the Authors' Association. She was a great joiner, and she knew everybody in the writing world in B.C. I knew her pretty well and socialized with her. She was fun.[8]

As soon as she arrived in Vancouver, Mildred joined the Vancouver Poetry Society (VPS). This was Canada's first poetry society (1916–1974), the first to produce a chapbook, the first to publish a magazine and the first to air a radio programme.[9] Mildred soon became a prominent personality holding the position of first vice-president (1936 to 1959) and honorary first vice-president until her death. In 1945, she was appointed as the Society's "representative at the inaugural and succeeding meetings of 'The Friends of the Public Library Association.'"[10] She actively participated in VPS activities, often serving as a guest speaker. During the 1935–1936 season, Mildred was one of the invited lecturers who, along with Dorothy Livesay, A.M. Stephen and John Vanderpant, "addressed the Society on subjects of much interest."[11] Her specific topics are unknown except for one delivered during the 1944–1945 season when it was reported her talk on "Indian people was received by a Vancouver audience with keen enthusiasm."[12] (Mildred was working as an amateur ethnologist, recording information on the aboriginal people she painted and their cultural activities and histories. She often shared that information via lectures.) Her appreciation for listening to poetry prompted her to join the newly formed Readers Group (1945–1946 season), whose purpose was to encourage "the art of reading poetry aloud."[13]

Untitled, n.d.
watercolour
8½" x 11½"
PRIVATE COLLECTION
DAN FAIRCHILD PHOTOGRAPHY

Within the VPS, Mildred met some famous personages (including poets Earle Birney and Al Purdy) and developed friendships with many, including the founding and thirty-year president Dr. Ernest Fewster, the noted Canadian photographer John Vanderpant and distinguished lawyer, writer and poet Thomas MacInnes (who was born in the same area of Ontario as Mildred). In 1957, the town of Dresden held a memorial for MacInnes, and Mildred's portrait of him was the "focal point of the celebration."[14] The next year, as part of Dresden's centennial celebrations, Mildred donated the portrait to the town; today, the painting hangs in the Dresden Public Library.

The VPS was popular, and a meeting could bring fifty or more members and numerous visitors. Meetings were often held in members' homes: Dr. Fewster's, the

Vanderpant Galleries (1216 Robson Street) and the Thornton household are those most often mentioned in the secretary's minutes. Special VPS parties were sometimes hosted by Mildred, and VPS records indicate that under her "guidance," the get-togethers were "carried through most successfully."[15]

On March 29, 1944, Mildred and MacInnes, members of the four-person radio committee, introduced *The Lyric West* on radio station CKMO, a fifteen-minute programme dedicated to poetry.[16] In the inaugural show, they gave a history of the VPS and read poems from some of the charter members. Whether she read her own work or that of other poets, Mildred aired on more than one programme; along with other members, she was described as having presented herself "forcibly and well."[17] Mildred was also on the selection committee for the Society's magazine, *Full Tide*. A person who always offered encouragement, along with a few others, she donated money for poetry awards for those submitting work to *Full Tide*.[18]

The Book of Days (1946), the only book published by the VPS, contains a brief history of the organization, short biographies of some of the members and an abbreviated anthology of their work. Presumably, due to Mildred's journalistic skills (she was by then the art critic for the *Vancouver Sun* and publishing articles in various newspapers and magazines), she wrote the historical overview of the Society. During her lifetime, Mildred published little poetry (some in newspapers and the *Saskatchewan Poetry Yearbook*, dates unknown), but "Three Totems" was included in *The Book of Days*.

The members of the VPS and the literary community recognized Mildred's talents as a painter. Several of her paintings were bestowed to members and important visitors. At a 1936 Canadian Authors' Association soiree in honour of poet Sir Charles G.D. Roberts (who was known as the Father of Canadian Poetry), attended by the VPS, one of Mildred's oil paintings was presented to Roberts.[19] On another occasion, John Murray Gibbon, the founding president of the Canadian Authors' Association and Canadian Pacific Railway publicity manager, was presented with Mildred's *Down Vancouver Way*, which depicted the Vancouver area mountains and a grain terminus. In 1942, Gibbon sent the painting to New York for inclusion in the Women's International Exposition of Arts and Industries.[20]

As if the VPS did not keep her busy enough, Mildred also became involved with the Totem-Land Society, a non-profit organization dedicated to "Foster and Protect Indian Arts and Promote Goodwill Among All Canadians."[21] The philosophy of the group was in keeping with her interests in preserving the traditional weaving, carving and painting of B.C.'s aboriginal peoples and in helping them attain full citizenship (which Mildred urged in several lectures and published articles). The Totem-Land Society was eventually subsumed by the Art, Historical and Scientific Association (to which Mildred also belonged), which later became the Vancouver Museum. Possibly, through one of these organizations, Mildred met and befriended the Kwakwaka'wakw carver Ellen Neel (1916–1966). Artists Charlie James, Mungo Martin and Ellen Neel have been credited with keeping the Kwakwaka'wakw (formerly known as Kwakiutl) style of carving from disappearing. Mildred's portrait of Neel's great-uncle, Mungo Martin is part of the McMichael Canadian Art Collection.

Ellen Neel and her family moved from Alert Bay to Vancouver in 1943. Shortly after, her husband, Ted, was handicapped by several strokes. The mother of six, Ellen became the breadwinner, turning her talents to designing, carving and painting totem poles. Ted was in charge of sales and, to achieve success, he and Ellen decided to develop totems for the tourist trade. Harry Duker was a founder of the Totem-Land Society and "a self-appointed, one-man publicity agent for the City of Vancouver." He commissioned Ellen to develop an insignia for the Totem-Land Society: a photogravure of a thunderbird sitting atop a globe that highlighted B.C.'s geographic features. Underneath kneeled a figure, representing the Thunderbird, giving the world to the first man. That image adorned the Society's letterhead and, along with others of Ellen's designs, was silkscreened onto "teeshirts, placemats, ties and scarves."[22] Prominent visitors to the city often departed with a Totem-Land tie, and VIPs were often given an Ellen Neel carving.

Through Harry Duker, the Neels set up a shop in Stanley Park, near the Pauline Johnson cairn at Ferguson Point, and started Totem Art Studios. There, during the summer, Ellen carved and painted totems while Ted sold them to eager tourists. Mildred frequented the park for nearby painting expeditions, visited the Neels from time to time and was supportive of Ellen's work and fortitude. Mildred understood

Mungo Martin (Kwakwaka'wakw), n. d. oil on board, 30" x 22" ORIGINAL IN McMICHAEL CANADIAN ART COLLECTION REPRODUCED FROM KODACHROME SLIDE IN THORNTON FAMILY PRIVATE COLLECTION, DIGITALLY RESTORED BY JANET DWYER

*Potlatch Houses
in Stanley Park*
(Squamish),1947
oil on board, 30" x 40"
ORIGINAL IN THE
McMICHAEL CANADIAN
ART COLLECTION
REPRODUCED FROM KODACHROME
SLIDE IN THORNTON FAMILY
PRIVATE COLLECTION, DIGITALLY
RESTORED BY JANET DWYER

Ellen's need to earn a living, as well as her talent. Ellen has been overlooked and sometimes treated dismissively because she and her family churned out souvenir totems in assembly-line fashion. For one 1965 commission, Ellen and her family completed five thousand small totems for the Hudson's Bay stores. In 1954, the local newspapers ran a story and photo of Ellen's son, David, amusingly breaking tradition by completing "the world's smallest totem" on which was carved a likeness of Bob Hope (which the celebrity was presented with when he visited Vancouver).[23] On the other hand, Ellen has been noted for preserving and reviving traditional Kwakwaka'wakw carving and for completing original designs. Included in her work was a sixteen-foot thunderbird totem for the University of British Columbia (UBC) Alma Mater Society in 1948, and she designed the foyer for the 1950 opening of the Harrison Hot Springs Hotel. For that job, she integrated "her traditional carvings within a decidedly contemporary setting."[24] One of Ellen's totem poles currently stands at Brockton Point in Stanley Park.

Mildred appreciated Ellen's carvings, and her home contained several examples. Moreover, Mildred's writings indicate the two women agreed that First Nations designs could beautify everyday items in non-aboriginal culture, including clothing, furniture and jewelry. Today, creations of artists such as Susan Point have worldwide markets but, during the 1940s and 1950s, such ideas were novel. There was little interest on the part of the non-aboriginal community in wearing aboriginal-designed jewelry or apparel. In 1954, Mildred attempted to make those designs more attractive to the general population. While exhibiting seventy-five First Nations portraits and ceremonial scenes at the Pacific National Exhibition, Mildred wore a jacket decorated with totem poles. The designs were iron-on transfers from the Haida and Kwakwaka'wakw peoples. The *Vancouver Sun*'s Edith Adams Cottage (an outlet that supplied textile patterns) sold the transfers in packets costing twenty-six cents.[25] Eight years earlier, in a 1946 *Vancouver Sun* article, Mildred suggested that work by First Nations artists should be encouraged: "Pottery, china, leather, metal and wood are just a few of the materials which could be enhanced by the application of Indian designs."[26] Photographs of purses and lapel ornaments from the Kainai (Blood)

Nation, a beaded belt and suitcase by Sadie Baker (Squamish Nation), a handbag bearing a Haida design and walking sticks from the Squamish Nation accompanied the article. Similarly, in a 1948 speech at a UBC conference on Native Indian Affairs, Ellen stressed that aboriginal art

> is a living symbol of... my people.... Our art continues to live, for not only is it part and parcel of us, but can be a powerful factor in combining the best part of Indian culture into the fabric of a truly Canadian art form.... We... must be allowed new and modern techniques... new and modern tools... [and] new and modern materials.... I believe it can be used to stunning effect on tapestry, textiles, sportswear and in jewellery. Many pieces of furniture lend themselves admirably to Indian designs. Public buildings, large restaurants and halls have already begun to utilize some of this art.[27]

When Ellen died in 1966, her friend Mildred stated,

> I admired her as a woman and honored and respected her as an artist.... She was a most self sacrificing [sic] woman who kept her family through her art. She was gentle, kind, and loving in every way as an individual.... A truly great and sincere artist... she was... a great credit to Canada and to her own people.[28]

Haida Totem Carver
circa 1945, oil on board
30" x 40"
REPRODUCED FROM KODACHROME
SLIDE IN THORNTON FAMILY
PRIVATE COLLECTION, DIGITALLY
RESTORED BY JANET DWYER

Indian Women Erecting Teepees, circa 1940
oil on canvas, 36" x 48"
REPRODUCED FROM KODACHROME
SLIDE IN THORNTON FAMILY
PRIVATE COLLECTION, DIGITALLY
RESTORED BY JANET DWYER

Whether to help the family financially or as a memento of her friend, after Ellen's death, Mildred purchased a totem pole of Ellen's that was approximately two feet high.

From 1944 to 1959, Mildred worked as the art critic for the *Vancouver Sun.* At age fifty-four, she happily undertook the position and visited exhibitions, wrote critiques and met deadlines until age sixty-nine. Jack notes that she was not paid much. A few years after settling in Vancouver, Mildred began writing book reviews (1939–1946). She covered music, poetry, fiction, non-fiction and children's publications. Like her later art reviews, her literary critiques were well-received. Canadian writer and social reformer A.M. Stephen said:

> May I tell you how much I appreciate your manner of writing…. It is difficult to condense one's general view of a book of poetry. You have done it admirably. I could use this, if modesty did not forbid, as an example in my class room [sic] when teaching literature.[29]

Mildred also published numerous articles in the *Native Voice* (1946–1969). The publication, founded in 1946 by Maisie Armytage Hurley, was Canada's first aboriginal newspaper and the official forum of the Native Brotherhood of B.C. (the province's first aboriginal group that concerned itself with First Nations rights). The publication was read across North America and was known for presenting "issues that no other newspaper or (later) TV channel would touch."[30] While Maisie was white, the editorial staff, directors and most contributors were aboriginal. Mildred, who along with Maisie was a member of the Native Sisterhood, often published reproductions of her First Nations portraits in this newspaper.

Prior to 1945, few non-aboriginals were concerned with the rights of First Nations. The participation of aboriginal soldiers in both world wars and an increased sensitivity worldwide to basic human rights helped develop a Canadian (and North American) consciousness of the concerns of aboriginal people. Maisie's husband, lawyer Tom Hurley, became well-known for defending B.C.'s First Nations people in criminal cases. Prior to her husband's death in 1961, Maisie would attend band meetings and volunteer his legal services for those in need of such assistance. B.C. lawyer and former judge of the Supreme Court of B.C., Thomas R. Berger described Maisie as "a tall, commanding woman… [and] a fierce defender of Aboriginal people's rights at a time when they were marginalized." With Tom's subtle and Maisie's more zealous encouragement, Berger also took on cases defending First Nations people. He recalls Maisie smacking her cane on his desk in 1963 and demanding, "'Now, Tommy, you will have to defend the Indians.'"[31] The case she was referring to was of two aboriginal men accused of shooting deer out of season. Berger persuaded the court that the conduct of the two accused was in fact entirely consistent with their aboriginal rights to hunt and fish for food.

Maisie was also an artist (thirteen of her pastel portraits of First Nations people are housed with the North Vancouver Museum and Archives). She inherited from her parents, and was personally given, numerous First Nations artifacts and art. Maisie hoped her collection would become part of a museum on the Capilano Reserve (Squamish Nation), but this never ocurred.[32] Not surprisingly, Mildred and Maisie became close: they had aboriginal friends in common, shared a sense of noblesse oblige and were early advocates for First Nations. In 1951, Mildred hosted the Hurley wedding lunch reception in her Comox Street home. In attendance were Chief and Mrs. Andy Frank (K'ómoks); Chiefs Isaac Jacobs, Dominique Charlie and August Jack Khatsahlano (Squamish); and Mrs. Angelo Branca. Several of Mildred's works formed a backdrop for the reception photograph, including the large painting *The Wedding of a Chief's Daughter*.[33]

As a result of her journalism, Mildred joined the Canadian Women's Press Club and was embraced by the group. Independent, intelligent and concerned with promoting journalism as a profession for women, the Club members focused on improving wages, working conditions and equal opportunities for female journalists. They believed that they had "a special role to interpret Canada to Canadians."[34] Their ideals and goals would have reinforced Mildred's desire to present her interpretations of First Nations life and Western Canada's landscapes to the country's citizenry.

The women were a lively group. Their camaraderie was shared during tea and dinner parties and, starting in 1947, the annual Fourth Estate Frolic (in 1957, the name changed to the Press Dance). In 1951, their male counterparts formed the Newsmen's Club and started to participate in the Frolics. Some of those men included the now-noted Canadian authors Barry Broadfoot and Pierre Berton and journalists Jack Wasserman and Jack Webster. Ticket sales were mainly used for philanthropic endeavours: sponsoring orphans, sending food packages to England after World War II and funding newspaper scholarships. Pat Carney, later a Conservative MP and senator, won the 1955 scholarship, which allowed her to work at the *Vancouver Province* for a year.[35]

Mildred had a role in the formation of the Fourth Estate Frolics. Business meetings were held in members' homes, and she hosted the March 1947 meeting. The members socialized amongst her paintings and aboriginal artifacts. All were in high spirits, and a dance was suggested.[36] The Frolics came to include songs, dances and humorous sketches. Mildred never participated in the routines, but the Club's records show she assisted with makeup, some introductions and other unnamed activities. The documentation in the City of Vancouver Archives indicates Mildred was an executive member in 1953, 1954 and 1958. When she died, a typed notation pasted into a Club scrapbook indicates how deeply Vancouver's female journalists cared for her: "Our Beloved Mildred Valley Thornton Has Left Us."[37] Several members attended Mildred's funeral and "pledged themselves to help carry out" [her] "long-held hope"[38] of keeping her aboriginal portrait collection in British Columbia. In a note to Jack Thornton, who was in the Royal Canadian Navy Reserve and living in Vancouver (Maitland was in the Royal Navy Reserve and living in England), journalist Myrtle Gregory asked if he was successful in interesting the B.C. Museum in Mildred's work "for the Indian wing." She also suggested "several... Press Club members would like to help if there is anything you would like us to do."[39] Neither Jack nor the Club members were successful in their aim of finding Mildred's First Nations portraits a home. In 1971, the Women's Press Club purchased and then donated the 1946 portrait of the renowned carver Chief Willie Sieweed (Seaweed in contemporary spelling) to the Vancouver Art Gallery. The first time the VAG exhibited the portrait was in 2003, thirty-two years after it had been acquired; since then, the portrait has been exhibited two more times.[40]

While she lived and painted in Vancouver, Mildred, a hard-working and energetic artist, led and participated in the development and maturation of important local and provincial art, cultural, literary and social groups. Her significant accomplishments during that time are a unique chronicle of a spirited and highly creative individual who believed deeply in contributing to the community she loved.

› *Willie Seaweed*
(Kwakwaka'wakw)
1946, oil on canvas
board, 30" x 22"
COLLECTION OF THE
VANCOUVER ART GALLERY,
GIFT OF THE CANADIAN
WOMEN'S PRESS CLUB,
VANCOUVER BRANCH
PHOTO: RACHAEL TOPHAM,
VANCOUVER ART GALLERY

Mildred Valley Thornton

FOUR

Buckskin and Advocacy

In the summer of 1928, Mildred read a newspaper story that was to change her life. The article described the birth of an aboriginal baby in a teepee on the Regina fairgrounds. Mildred wanted to see the "little papoose." A few days later, with her nearly three-year-old twins in tow, she made her way to the aboriginal encampment at the fairgrounds. When she found the teepee, she explained that she wished to see the newborn. Once inside, she was infatuated by the infant. The people in the teepee were just as taken with Jack and Maitland, who were dressed identically. She noted that she "had provided a treat for them while they furnished one for me. It was a fair exchange."[1] That idea of reciprocity stayed with Mildred and became central to her dealings with First Nations people. Unlike some other painters of her era, Mildred always paid her aboriginal models for their time. Additionally, when she came to know certain people, she would provide them with items they desired, such as tobacco or tins of salmon.

‹ Mildred Valley Thornton
circa 1950
THORNTON FAMILY
PRIVATE COLLECTION
PHOTOGRAPHER UNKNOWN

Mildred related that the experience in the teepee and "the color and character" of all she saw at the encampment motivated her to return. The next day she found someone to watch the boys and finally launched her career as a portrait painter of First Nations people. It had been fifteen years since she had felt artistically inspired by the sight of a Plains Indian, stately in regalia, standing on the platform of the Regina railway station. When she saw Peter Weasel-Skin serenely sitting in front of his teepee, smoking a pipe, she had her first subject. They could not speak each other's languages, but Mildred never found that a hindrance, as there was "one tongue all could understand—the language of the heart." With his approval, Mildred started painting. Weasel-Skin was soon oblivious to her presence, but others nearby were not. Mildred found the onlookers repeatedly "thrusting their heads so close to my paint box that I could hardly get my brush in for a refill." She was always a good sport about such adversities, stressing, "Difficult as it made my task I would not spoil their fun and worked furiously to capture as best I could the placid features of my subject." Like those crowded round, Peter Weasel-Skin was amazed when he viewed his likeness "and more astonished still" when Mildred paid him.[2]

That day, Mildred also painted a man called Strong Eagle. In the hundreds of aboriginal portraits to follow, she worked as she had on those first two, painting "Indians wherever I found them, in whatever they were wearing, with an absolute disregard of formality or prearranged plan."[3] By working that way, she broke from the portraiture tradition of studio sittings. She painted people in such places as fields, barns and in their beds. Instead of working in a comfortable studio over a series of sittings, Mildred usually had one opportunity and a limited time to capture the likenesses and character of her subjects.

After that fortuitous day in Regina, Mildred went home not knowing "the first inhabitants of our beloved land, could so creep into my heart as to possess it utterly, and the one compelling urge of my life should be to record as much as I could of their fleeting history."[4] The whereabouts of those first two portraits is unknown, and they may have been culled or sold: although she had been painting First Nations people for over a decade, not until the early 1940s does she seem to have decided to preserve that work as a historical record. She became convinced that the faces and stories of our First Nations "should be fitted into their place in Canadian tradition."[5] She hoped one day to have her "Collection" preserved by a museum or art gallery. In addition, paintings filled her home, and for several decades, she paid to keep the bulk of them housed at the fireproof Vancouver Safety Vaults. Resolute, no obstacle deterred Mildred from her vocation.

Mildred found aboriginal people interesting because they were the country's first inhabitants. From the very start, her mission was to paint exceptional personages from communities in B.C., Alberta and Saskatchewan. Initially, she focused her attention on older chiefs, artists and the relatives of important leaders. Over time, she turned her brushes to anyone she found intriguing. She painted "on-the-spot"[6] while gathering first-hand information about the various persons and populations. Mildred originally thought that North America's aboriginal peoples were dying out, a common idea at the beginning of the twentieth century; she later became a champion for their political and spiritual rights, educational opportunities and improved living conditions.

Nuxalk Chief, 1945
oil on board, 30" x 25"
PRIVATE COLLECTION
JOHN CAMERON PHOTOGRAPHY

Mildred came to realize that the effects of reserve life, residential schools, the banning of religious ceremonies—such as the Sun Dance and potlatches—and Western culture in general were eradicating or changing many important aboriginal traditions and rituals. Like several artists before her, she undertook the task of documenting aboriginal people and their songs, dances and stories. She used her journalism skills to both enlighten and advocate, publishing articles on First Nations art, customs, issues and individuals. She also gave illustrated presentations to numerous groups over the years, including such diverse bodies as the B.C. Teacher-Librarians Association, parent-teacher associations, the Social Credit Women's Auxiliary, the Vancouver Poetry Society and historical groups.

Under the auspices of the Association of Canadian Clubs, in 1945, 1946 and 1947,

Medicine Man (Piikani),
titled 'Piegan' in
previous publications
n.d., oil on board
14" x 10¾"
PRIVATE COLLECTION
WESTBRIDGE PHOTOGRAPH

Mildred lectured to groups across B.C. and the country. These were rigorous undertakings in which, almost daily, she reached new destinations via busses, ferries or trains. In one unpublished account, she complained that on the train ride from North Battleford to Prince Albert, Saskatchewan, there was "smoke everywhere [and] no place to eat."[7] Such discomforts were not enough to deter Mildred because, as she pointed out, "If I can create a better understanding of the Canadian Indians, I feel I have done my part towards eliminating racial prejudice towards these noble people."[8] At a time when First Nations people were negatively stereotyped, Mildred declared her respect and admiration for them. She explained that the purpose of her lectures was to fulfill her "earnest desire" to create "more understanding and service toward these, your fellow Canadians."[9]

In 1947, her topic was "Indians as I Have Known Them," and she drew huge audiences, filling such venues as the ballroom of the Hotel Vancouver[10] and a large private dining room in the Hotel Saskatchewan. Her young friend Reg Ashwell recalled that, after one lecture, the audience of approximately three hundred gave Mildred a standing ovation.[11] In 1954, Mildred again lectured across the country, as far as Halifax; and in 1959, she gave several illustrated talks in London, England.

Kodachrome slides of her work accompanied most of Mildred's presentations. A tape recording of one address indicates that drumming, recorded during her travels to First Nations communities, introduced Mildred's presentations. She described the differences between various tribes, and with each portrait, she told anecdotes that highlighted the character and experiences of the sitter. When an individual was of historical importance, she stressed that his or her story was significant to Canada's cultural heritage. Mildred also described customs and beliefs particular to each community.

While she respected aboriginal people, was genuine in her attempts to advocate on their behalf and successfully represented them in new and non-stereotypical ways, at times Mildred unwittingly transgressed cultural boundaries. Her "role as 'message bearer' or 'spokesperson' for Native people was problematic; her voice was heard over those of First Nations people themselves, who might have defined issues concerning their communities in very different terms."[12] Although Mildred retold First Nations myths and stories as a way to improve understanding and empathy between cultures, that practice is sometimes considered an act of cultural appropriation if done without the agreement of the Nation. Deborah Jacobs, the Squamish Nation Education Director, explains:

> The public needs to hear the narratives and stories of First Nations people from the First Nations voice; while Mildred wanted to share that, I don't believe she applied any protocols for sharing. She was told a story in the moment… not so she could write a book about it or pass it on.[13]

Mildred's views were those of one who resided outside the culture. While she befriended, empathized with and championed their interests, Mildred could never fully understand the plight and desires of aboriginal people. Mildred is distinct, however, in that she did not use her First Nations portraits as a means to promote her career as did some other artists such as the American George Catlin (1796–1872) and Canada's Paul Kane (1810–1871) who exploited "the exotic appeal of Native people."[14] Unlike Kane, she avoided European-style romanticism in her work. Furthermore, as pointed out by Daniel Francis, Kane often "manipulated" the settings and landscapes of his work and sometimes added "clothing and artifacts foreign to the Indians in the paintings." In this way he used them "as exotic curiosities."[15] Mildred, on the other hand, always strove for mutual exchange, collaboration and education, as opposed to personal profit or exploitation.

In the twentieth-first century, Canadians reside in a multicultural society. While far from being free of racism, life today is vastly different from that of the early part of the twentieth century. During that time, novels, movies and art supported views of aboriginals as either childlike or noble savages—the portrayal of the "imaginary Indian" was popular and exploited.[16] At the same time, negative and stereotypical views of aboriginal people were even more plentiful than today. For instance, in 1956, a United Church of Canada report described aboriginal people living on reserves as having, among other things, "excessive laziness… lack of understanding, and appreciation of the value of money… and lack of personal initiative."[17] First Nations were decimated by disease and the physical and psychological abuses of residential schools, and their voices were often ignored or suppressed. Treated paternalistically, they were not allowed to vote federally until 1960 (B.C. First Nations gained the provincial vote in 1947).

In her role as journalist, Mildred published informative articles on aboriginal life in newspapers across the country. Language that would be deemed unacceptable today was commonplace during Mildred's era, and her writings indicate that she, too, sometimes unintentionally patronized or romanticized. Above all, Mildred intended her stories to be respectful, illuminating and a means to debunking stereotypes. In 1946, she informed the public that "no longer is the Indian a 'vanishing Canadian.'" She also pointed out that, while the eye disease trachoma was being eradicated with sulfa drugs and prenatal care was improving child mortality rates in First Nations, tuberculosis was still a threat. Mildred reported that new hospitals and better health care were reducing the number of tubercular patients, but she cautioned (in what now seems a huge understatement) there was "still room for improvement."[18]

In 1950, one year prior to decriminalization of the potlatch in B.C., Mildred published "Indian Aristocracy" in the *Vancouver Sun*. She discussed social hierarchy among the West Coast peoples, the importance of heraldry and totem poles and the skirmishes and taking of slaves that had sometimes occurred historically. Many in First Nations communities turned to Mildred for assistance, and she included a letter from the Kwakwaka'wakw chief, Tom Johnson. He asked Mildred, a member of the Native Sisterhood, to print the letter to inform non-aboriginals about the importance of ancient customs.

> Dear Sister, We are sending you this letter to put our words to the newspaper. We want to let everyone know that we have not sold our birthright. It is only right to save some of our songs, dances, masks and legends.
>
> The time is growing short when such things can be recorded at all. It is important to save what we can before it is too late. A few brief years and memory

Arriving at the Potlatch
(Squamish), circa 1940
oil on board, 30" x 40"
PRIVATE COLLECTION
DAN FAIRCHILD PHOTOGRAPHY

of the old songs, dances and legends shall have passed away…. At the time the Indian Act was enforced re the potlatch, the Kwakiutl agency was asked to surrender all our masks, coppers, and blankets… to Ottawa.

We did not surrender them, but went to jail…. Those that did surrender theirs… are making new ones.

Mildred concluded the article by telling readers, "Rules of etiquette and behavior are very strictly enforced in the many governments of the world. It is quite proper that the Indians, too, should have their own procedure, and take pride in their old traditions."[19]

After providing a short history of the people in "Totems Fall, But Haidas Thrive," Mildred explained in her *Vancouver Sun* magazine supplement article that

the might and mystery of their enchanted surroundings were reflected in the inventive genius of the race, giving rise not only to a rich and almost inexhaustible fund of legend and folklore, but also producing some of the finest native art in existence.[20]

Chief Money Bird (Cree)
1930, oil on board
24″ x 18″
THORNTON FAMILY
PRIVATE COLLECTION
PHOTO BY JANET DWYER

Manitouwassis (Cree)
1929, oil on canvas
35″ x 26″
PRIVATE COLLECTION
DAN FAIRCHILD PHOTOGRAPHY

She went on to laud the people of Massett on Haida Gwaii (then called the Queen Charlotte Islands) for putting in their own water system. She did lament that dental care was poor and that the community would be better off returning to the diet of their ancestors.

Mildred also noted that, in Haida Gwaii, Charley Gladstone was the only remaining goldsmith and Captain Andrew Brown was the sole argillite carver. She cautioned, "It is a great pity that these distinctive arts are not being developed by the younger people…. It would be a grave cultural loss should they disappear."[21] Fortunately, carvers and painters like Charlie James, Judith P. Morgan, Ellen Neel, Mungo Martin and, later, Bill Reid inspired and influenced younger artists whose work today is valued worldwide. Mildred hoped for such a resurgence. Besides newspaper articles, she wrote on First Nations art for specialized audiences in such publications as the

Canadian Antiques Collector and *Museum and Art Notes*. In the latter, she declared, "British Columbia may proudly claim to have perhaps the most unique and virile form of native art in the whole world." She went on to urge:

> We must restore to the Indian that pride in his traditions and in his native gifts which has been largely lost through the painful process of assimilation; in so doing we shall build up confidence, self respect [sic] and happiness…. Many, very many of the old arts and crafts are gone forever, but some still remain, and these constitute a very real part of our natural wealth. We should regard Indian art as a national asset.[22]

One can only assume how pleased Mildred would be to know that First Nations art is now showcased throughout the country, that First Nations were an integral part of the 2010 Winter Olympics and that the work of the aboriginal peoples of Canada now commands international attention.

Mildred's writings often highlighted the talents or achievements of B.C. aboriginal leaders like Billy Assu of Cape Mudge, Chief George of Sechelt, Chief Mathias Joe of the Squamish Nation and their prairie counterparts such as Manitouwassis, Chief Shot-on-Both-Sides and Chief Walking Buffalo. In 1950, she lauded Frank Calder, Canada's first aboriginal MLA (1949), for his intelligence and oratory skills at the twentieth convention of the Native Brotherhood. She described the event as "a blending… of ancient wisdom and modern knowledge."[23] Mildred also discussed and praised the crafts, cuisine and hospitality of the convention's Nuxalk hosts. In addition, she published narratives on interesting couples like Mr. and Mrs. Pat Cappo and Dominic and Louise Jack. Because aboriginal women always intrigued Mildred, she also chronicled the lives and personalities of several, including Mary Capilano (Squamish), Annie Dawson (Haida) and Mary Dick (Ntlakyapamuk, earlier referred to as Thompson River).

Mildred published two articles in 1950 on an unusual drama for the era. *Tzinquaw* was an operatic presentation of a Cowichan legend of the Thunderbird (Tzinquaw) and the Killer Whale. People from the Cowichan Nation not only approved, twenty-

Mildred in regalia, n.d.
THORNTON FAMILY
PRIVATE COLLECTION
PHOTOGRAPHER UNKNOWN

Qu'Appelle Valley, n.d.
oil on board, 9⅝" x 19⅝"
PRIVATE COLLECTION
DAN FAIRCHILD PHOTOGRAPHY

five members of the community formed the cast. Mildred noted, "It will be a revelation to white people to discover how much talent is hidden away on the reserves."[24]

Because of her sympathetic support, several First Nations individuals and communities looked to Mildred to represent them. At least four clans gave her honorary names, which she cherished. In making her a princess of the Eagle Clan, Kwakwaka'wakw Chief Charley Nowell named her "Ah-ou-Mookht," which Mildred understood to mean "The one who wears a blanket because she is of noble birth." The mother of Chief Stanislaus Almighty Voice (Cree) dubbed her "Owas-ka-ta-esk-ean," which Mildred said meant "Putting your most ability for us Indians." Her friend, Nuxalk chief Jim Pollard, named her "Quol-kla-cum," an old term for people who made pictures; and she also had a Sitsika (Blackfoot) name, "Mo-jai-sin-a-ki."

Mildred somehow acquired the buckskin dress of the famous early Métis poet Pauline Johnson (1861–1913), who gave readings across Canada while dressed in the regalia of a Métis princess. As Johnson traveled to remote locales, Mildred may have seen one of Johnson's performances. Besides her poetry, Mildred likely also admired Johnson's fervent nationalism. For her lectures, Mildred wore dresses of smoked buckskin—a creamy yellow colour—trimmed with fringe and beads made of tiny deer hooves. Another outfit, presented to her by the Eagle Clan, is a huge dark-blue blanket, trimmed with mother of pearl and beads and with this goes a carved wooden mask. Her most elaborate costume, which she is wearing for her speeches across Canada [for the Canadian Club], is of white doeskin, beautifully fringed and beaded. The Assiniboine Indians presented it to her, especially for the lecture tour."[25]

Chief Jim Crow Flag
(Piikani), 1949
oil on board
24" x 18"
PRIVATE COLLECTION
JOHN CAMERON PHOTOGRAPHY

There may be differing opinions amongst First Nations on whether non-aboriginal people should wear regalia. As Deborah Jacobs of the Squamish Nation points out, such outfits are "very special" and are used for specific purposes by the First Nations. Mildred

was gifted [dresses and blankets] by different families. With that gift, came the right and the expectation that she was going to use them at some point. [While] she was lecturing in buckskin dress... she wasn't saying she was from that Nation.... Our elders used to give things to non-native people, or they would trade and barter for service; so, it was felt that [the exchange] was fair. From that perspective, the integrity or the dignity and the respect was mutual.[26]

While sometimes declaring that she wished she had been born a Canadian Indian, Mildred never pretended to be one. During her lectures, she usually appeared in a buckskin dress and beaded doeskin moccasins. She also often wore silver bracelets and earrings or a beaded headband with one or two feathers and various necklaces of beads, claws and porcupine quills that had been made by aboriginal artisans. A buckskin dress was given to her by her friend Chief Dan Kennedy-Ochankugahe (who was also a journalist well-known to Saskatchewan First Nations) for her 1947 cross-country Canadian Club tour. Afterwards, Kennedy wrote Mildred from his home on the Assiniboine Reserve in Montmartre, Saskatchewan:

Congratulations for your successful tour of the Dominion in the interests of Art and our cause. You have done a magnificent job as our ambassador of good will. I have watched your progress… like a meteor across the Dominion. Our only regret is that the dress is unfinished. It would require another three or four weeks to finish the beadwork on the sleeves above the fringes. If you would ship it back to us, my wife will put the finishing touches on it.[27]

During her well-enunciated lectures, in her clear, strong voice Mildred emphasized:

I make no apologies for appearing before you in an Indian costume. I wear it as a reminder of the artistic gifts, character, and resourcefulness of a great people…. As one who is proud to be called Canadian I wish to speak a word for that great and silent company of original Canadians to whom we owe so much and of whom we are largely unaware…. I have gone alone, and entirely unaided among the various tribes… painting outstanding characters and types and meeting with the most unfailing courtesy, kindness and hospitality…. The more I went among these people, the better I understood them, and the better I understood them, the more I loved them…. A portion of my collection has been photographed in kodachrome [sic]… Some of these are excellent reproductions—others are not… but all of them will give you an idea of the poise, dignity, and general characteristics of the people I have painted.

Only a youngster at the time, Lance Evoy has never forgotten the powerful presence of his great-aunt on the lecture stage in Dresden, Ontario.

I remember being in the hall with the lights down, [and] this incredible figure up there speaking. She showed slides that evening, but all I can remember is her standing on that stage by herself looking out into the [packed] audience, this amazing figure in a white buckskin dress. That dress was striking, and she came across as almost magical. After the lecture, many people gathered around her. I remember going up with my mother and Aunt Millie signing my mother's programme. My brother and I were always told what a distinguished person Aunt Millie was, how important she was in the family, and how happy people were for her artistic success. Seeing her at that lecture resonated with me.[28]

Mildred was also memorable for journalist Augustus Brindle who stated that, during her talks, she "kept the interest so intense, that people forgot all about time. Her chats during refreshments were even more beguiling."[29]

With talks that were always aimed at increasing understanding of and respect for our First Nations population, Mildred lectured:

> Religion was the real life of the tribes, permeating all their activities and ceremonies. No enterprise was ever undertaken without prayer, fasting, and cleansing.... I think there could be few lovelier things than to see an old Indian man, perhaps some old patriarch of the tribe, take a newborn infant outside and hold it up to the sun in reverent prayer, that it might be guided and blessed by the Great Spirit. This used to be a common custom on the plains and is infrequently done today.

Ruth Standing Alone
(Kainai), 1942
oil on board, 17" x 14½"
REPRODUCED FROM KODACHROME
SLIDE IN THORNTON FAMILY
PRIVATE COLLECTION, DIGITALLY
RESTORED BY JANET DWYER

During her addresses, Mildred conveyed her admiration of the "love of color" and "sense of design" found in aboriginal art. She described First Nations artists as "wonderfully inventive and "ingenious in their work." In addition, after outlining their customs and lifestyles, Mildred cautioned that, in the first half of the twentieth century, Canada's First Nations were "in a sense a people without a country, without hope, without a future, and of course this has a demoralizing effect." Prior to their receiving the franchise, she regularly argued that aboriginal Canadians should have the right to vote: "Who can doubt that they have... the things that are required for noble and useful citizenship?" She also reminded non-aboriginals of the courage and patriotism of the First Nations: "Thousands of Indians were in the front lines of Canada's battlefields.... In 1942 alone they contributed over $400,000 in cash to the war effort."[30] According to newspaper accounts, during her 1947 lecture tour, Mildred also chided that it was incorrect to "keep them shut away on reserves" and then "bring them out for show."[31] Fifteen years after World War II, as indicated in a photograph in the *Native Voice*, Mildred was still using her celebrity as a "prominent Vancouver artist" to highlight and support aboriginal military personnel as she posed with the First Nations crew of HMS *Excellent*.[32]

Mildred continually advocated for better educational opportunities, but her personality and background blinded her to the hardships of residential schooling. Raised in an era when children did chores and had strict upbringings, she believed that the early hours (sometimes 3:00 or 4:00 AM) and the work activities of residential schools would be good for every school child. The same woman who washed little Kae MacLean's face so vigorously seems to have considered some hardship a necessary price for the education she deemed vital for aboriginal youth. Furthermore, a mother who could leave her own offspring for months may not have understood the misery caused by school-related removal from families. Yet, in *Ruth Standing Alone* (painted at St. Paul's Residential School, Cardston, Alberta, 1942), Mildred conveyed a heart-wrenching portrait.

During her oratories, Mildred insisted that educators had the "power to mould character, to create ideals, and to lay enduring foundations for life." Just as importantly, Mildred viewed education as a vital "help in erasing prejudice and building up in its place intelligent understanding and those true images which make for progress and happiness." Mildred later recommended that

> Indian children... [should] attend the same schools as our own children and mingle with them on terms of the fullest equality. Here in the city we have dozens of different nationalities... all being educated with our own children. Why should the Indians who surely have a prior right to such privileges be excluded?

She further argued that society's hiring practices should change, chiding that "Too often aboriginal people "come up against a blank wall of indifference and neglect among white people." She asked why "an educated Indian girl… [or] boy was not being given 'an equal right' to professional careers with his [or her] non-Indian counterparts if they have 'equal ability.'"

Mildred asked difficult questions and struggled to make the non-aboriginal population have "an awakened consciousness." During lectures she railed:

> Many of these dear people are oppressed by frustration, loss of self-respect, and a sense of inferiority. This is what we have done to them—not the government, nor the Indian department,—but you, and you, and you…. Let us determine to undo the ills of which we are guilty. Let us shake off our indifference and apathy, and render to these, our fellow-Canadians, the full mead of friendship, interest, and cooperation, which it is our duty and privilege to give.

After such a scolding, Mildred then proceeded with her slide show of portraits and ceremonial scenes.

Mildred hoped for what is beginning to occur today. Besides undergoing an artistic renaissance, Canada's First Nations are beginning to take control of their lives. A few treaties are being signed, individual communities are becoming self-governing, and increasingly non-aboriginal Canadians are, as Mildred suggested, "eager to atone for the past, and to extend the hand of true brotherhood." She foresaw that when First Nations had "fullest equality" they would "quickly demonstrate… their own special gifts and endowments to enrich the human, cultural and spiritual life" of our country.[33] Her work is now "an important window onto interpretations of Canadian history, relationships between Whites and aboriginal people, and the notion of a Canadian identity itself."[34]

Blue Wings (Piikani)
1942, oil on board
20" x 16"
PRIVATE COLLECTION
DAN FAIRCHILD PHOTOGRAPHY

FIVE

Capturing a Page of History

Her affection for Canada's indigenous peoples and their art caused Mildred to surround herself with examples of their work. Her home became museum-like, filled with baskets, drums, masks, paddles and totem poles that were either purchased or given to her. Mildred wrote that her obsession with all things aboriginal made her think she could possibly have been one in another life. At some point, Mildred painted a self-portrait in which she wore a First Nations headdress. In so doing, she might also have been acknowledging her Indian names. The self portrait could have reflected Mildred's interest in Pauline Johnson, with whom Mildred seems to have felt a special connection. Another explanation is that Mildred may have been portraying a wistful and symbolic image of herself: after all, "underlying all self-portraiture is the mystery of how an individual sees himself or herself as other. A self-portrait involves an artist objectifying their own body and creating a 'double' of themselves." In portraying herself in regalia, Mildred could have been expressing her affinity with and respect for First Nations. Her eyes are dreamy, yet inviting, and she appears to be in a transcendent state. The image entices the viewer to look deeply and beyond the surface representation. The painting may also have been a

‹ *Self-Portrait,* n.d.
oil on canvas, 24" x 20"
KEITH AND JUDY SCOTT
PRIVATE COLLECTION
DAN FAIRCHILD PHOTOGRAPHY

Mildred and John
circa 1955, living room
of house at 1771 Comox
Street, Vancouver
THORNTON FAMILY
PRIVATE COLLECTION
PHOTOGRAPHER UNKNOWN

symbolic attempt to link two cultures. Like all good portraiture, Mildred's self-portrait is both subtle and powerful: "a metaphorical mirror" that makes her depiction "both compelling and elusive."[1]

Mildred's choice of artistic subjects was not an easy one. Few people, including her aging mother (Mildred's father had died in 1929), understood why Mildred wanted to leave the comforts of her home, family and studio to go "chasing those wild Indians all over the country when there were plenty of white people to paint." Although she did not tell her mother this, Mildred's response was, "In the main, my own race seemed to me a dull, expressionless lot compared to the Indians and did not interest me sufficiently."[2]

In order to paint her subjects, Mildred wrote that she needed

physical endurance. The qualities of a good packhorse often seemed more important than intellectual equipment. Starting out on a trip with perhaps twenty or more boards to carry, as well as my heavy paint box, my suit case, and in later years also a projector, slides and screen to show the Indians what I had done, required the limit of my strength.[3]

When her boys were younger, Mildred had no option but to take them with her on painting trips. She explained, "Babysitters are a modern innovation… you took 'em or you stayed home."[4] Jack remembers that he and Maitland

went with her a couple of times when she couldn't palm us off on anyone else. We stayed overnight in teepees…. I recall there were palliasses [mattresses filled with straw or other resilient material]. We thought it was amazing the Indians could make a fire in a teepee. I don't think we slept very much because it was all too exciting. Some of the Indian men made us little bows and arrows and showed us how to use them. They thought it was amusing that my brother and I didn't know how to make a campfire and that, unlike the Indian children, we weren't aware of the simplest tools of life. Maitland and I thought it was all tremendously interesting.

While the boys played, Jack recalls that their mother would be sitting on her collapsible stool, somewhere in the encampment, painting. Having small boys in tow, Mildred said she "had to paint with one eye on my canvas and the other on the youngsters. This was good exercise for the eyes, but rough on the nerves."[5]

One of Mildred's favourite portraits, and one of her best, was of a Cree woman in a Saskatchewan encampment circa 1940. Mrs. Rock Thunder was "peacefully smoking a pipe" outside her tent.[6] Mildred enjoyed the twinkle in the woman's eyes, which she successfully captured in the study. Mildred sent Marius Barbeau, the famed Canadian ethnologist, a print reproduction of the painting, telling him that Mrs. Rock Thunder

> could not speak a word of English and I could not speak a word of Cree, but I showed her some money and my paint box. She merely nodded, so I sat right down on the ground then and there and painted furiously, in case she might take off. That is the way it has always been, working under great pressure, never knowing what lay ahead, and never caring, so long as I could do the job in hand.[7]

The portrait was completed in less than an hour, using "every ounce of energy" Mildred had.[8]

Mildred always worked quickly. An hour is a long time for any sitter. For that reason, most portrait subjects must endure several sittings. Mildred usually had only one opportunity with her aboriginal subjects and always feared that her sitters would become tired or bored. She usually used charcoal for her initial quick sketch and then always "concentrated on the face, making hasty indications of color and design in the clothing" that she could finish later.[9]

One story related by Reg Ashwell indicates Mildred's talent under difficult conditions and the "indomitable spirit and fantastic energy [that] never failed her." Mildred had just been in hospital for a "painfully unpleasant"[10] treatment of phlebitis, or the leukemia-like blood disorder that eventually took her life, but she was anxious to travel to Vancouver Island. There, she wanted to paint Chief Jimmy John (Tah-ai-Suym), a highly regarded Nuu-chah-nulth (formerly Nootka) carver and a relative of famous Chief Maquinna.[11] When Reg suggested she recover for a week or two, Mildred replied that Jimmy John was "already quite old and time is running out if I'm ever going to do it." They set off with Reg's "little car loaded down with her oils and canvasses [and boards], as well as her projector and kodachromes."[12]

Mary George, "Old Mary" (Cowichan) circa 1943, oil on board, 20" x 14"
PRIVATE COLLECTION
DAN FAIRCHILD PHOTOGRAPHY

Mrs. Rock Thunder (Cree), circa 1940 oil on canvas, 20" x 17"
PRIVATE COLLECTION
DAN FAIRCHILD PHOTOGRAPHY

Jimmy John did not speak English, so his son, Leslie, did the translating. At first, Jimmy John refused Mildred's request. She knew how to charm and asked if he would like to view her slides. Reg recounts that the old man "was completely won over and wished to be painted immediately and join the ranks of those thus immortalized, like the Kwakiutl [Kwakwaka'wakw] chief Billy Assu and Chief Mathias Joe Capilano."[13] Donning a headdress of red cedar and copper bands with long white fur pelts, Jimmy John was ready. However, he was not a patient subject. Reg laughed:

> I'll never forget that experience as long as I live. Mildred was busy painting him, and he was sitting there serenely…. Right in the middle of painting his portrait, with Mildred's brushes going furiously,… all of a sudden… Jimmy sprang to his feet and he whirled around that room, you'd think he was about twenty-five years old. The ermine tails were flying around and his cloak flying out like a big fan. It put her off her stroke, but she never let on. She just went right on painting him.[14]

After a mere twenty-five minutes, Jimmy John declared the painting session was over. For Reg, "the speed with which Mildred worked was nothing short of amazing, as her brush fairly flew over the canvas. The perspiration was actually dripping from her face, no doubt because of the extreme effort of concentration."[15]

Jimmy John's portrait conveys his status, pride and confidence. His face is strong and determined, and he has a dignified presence. Reg said the painting is somewhat deceptive: the Chief seems tall, but he was actually a short man. Mildred has him fill the canvas in order to emphasize his renown and powerful personality. Out of necessity, her brushstrokes are freer than those observed in Mrs. Rock Thunder's portrait.

Some reviewers have criticized Mildred's brushstrokes. In 1990, one wrote that Mildred "did not bring a developed technical skill to her work," nor did she "have a fine brushstroke or a style which can stand the test of time."[16] In contrast, commercial gallery owners like Gunter Heinrich of Winchester Galleries in Victoria, B.C., find her landscapes "competent," with "a nice sensitivity to light." He further points out, "You couldn't achieve what she did if you had bad brushstrokes." In terms of Mildred's portraiture, Heinrich says figurative painting is not appreciated in North America and stresses that more than a likeness is necessary, emphasizing that Mildred's portraits "were fabulously done. She absolutely captured the person."[17]

Art specialist Uno Langmann concurs, noting that Mildred worked with large brushes, and

> she had a very, very loose hand. To make a painting with a wide brush, you have to be very sure where you put your brush; very few people can do that. Mildred was much like Emily Carr in her self-assuredness. Mildred managed to capture the ultimate feeling that she saw in her sitters—their souls.[18]

Another of Mildred's more compelling images, and one that has stood the test of time, is the study of the Squamish ancestor Siyámlut, or "Aunt Polly." Her great-"grandniece" points out that, while the painting is not a mirror image, the portrait reminds her "of things people have said about Tata Polly's character or attitude."[19]

Chief Jimmy John
(Nuu-chah-nulth)
circa 1963
oil on board
30" x 22"
PRIVATE COLLECTION
JOHN CAMERON PHOTOGRAPH

Siyámlut ("Aunt Polly")
(Squamish), 1940
oil on board, 24" x 22"
UNO LANGMANN
PRIVATE COLLECTION
DAN FAIRCHILD PHOTOGRAPHY

Langmann considers *"Aunt Polly,"* one of the few First Nations portraits Mildred painted on canvas, to be one of her best depictions. Mildred herself said, "Seldom have I been so completely absorbed in painting anyone as I was in doing Siamelaht [Siyámlut in contemporary spelling]." In her nineties, the elder was frail but still indulged in the favoured pastime of pipe smoking. Mildred could not abide smoking, but wanted to portray her subject in this natural activity. After settling the old woman comfortably in her bed, Mildred had a predicament: Siyámlut's "pipe lay on a chair beside the bed. I looked at it hopefully but hesitated to ask her to smoke it, as some of these old folk are exceedingly sensitive and, not for worlds, would I offend one of them." After a friend who had accompanied Mildred offered the old woman a cigarette, Siyámlut proceeded to chew it. Not enjoying that experience, the elder finally picked up her pipe. Mildred described the woman's face as "calm, resolute and full of character." The portrait successfully conveys "the page of history which was revealed" to Mildred "written" on the old woman's face. Besides paying her, Mildred provided Siyámlut with a "sizeable donation of the noxious weed" when she next visited.[20]

Mildred made many friends in various First Nations communities. One was the noted Haida carver Mark Spence. Mildred not only corresponded with Spence in the last year of his life, but she tried "to solicit interest in his work [and] to help him sell his carvings." On November 10, 1944, Spence wrote to say that he would send Mildred a thirty-inch totem pole she wanted to purchase if, in return, she would buy him a hat from a Vancouver shop. He explained, "Lots of holes in this old hat now."[21] Mildred was happy to do so. Four days later, Spence wrote to say the small totem was finished.

Margaret Locke was a young girl when Mildred visited people on Squamish lands. She recalls, "Mildred was around frequently in the summer." She also remembers that Mildred "loved my grandaunt," Chucháwlut (Maryanne August), and that many of the Squamish elders liked Mildred: "She was a very nice, very nice lady. She was not prejudiced. She was right at home when she was with the Natives. She was quiet and soft spoken." Mildred also usually packed a lunch, and she would often "bring extra" to share or, sometimes, even gave away her own meal.[22]

One August afternoon in 1940, Mildred was strolling through the Squamish reserve looking for individuals to paint. She asked two men to sit for her, but both declined. Then she saw Chucháwlut [Chuchoweleth to Mildred], who "was much over ninety,"[23] seated outside her door. At first, the elder refused Mildred's request because another painter had kept Chucháwlut longer than stated and had not given her the canvas as promised. With genuine admiration, Mildred commented on the beauty of the elderly woman's long black braids. Chucháwlut "was very proud of her braids,"[24] and the compliment softened her resolve. Mildred indicated a half-hour on her watch, and "held up some money." Chucháwlut consented, and in just ten minutes beyond the allotted half-hour (for which she was paid extra), Mildred had captured the "tiny, delicate ears and small, shapely hands." She also portrayed a mouth that "was full and round and boasted lovely curves."[25] Mildred further conveyed the vigor of an elder who, according to her grandniece, "didn't have hearing problems. She never wore glasses. She'd thread her own needle. In January, she'd wash her hair outside." Mildred's depiction also reflected Chucháwlut's fun-loving nature. Margaret Locke says the portrait causes her "to get all choked up. It is very special. Auntie was very close to us. There aren't many photographs of her."[26]

Her ability to make friends in various First Nations communities seems to have stemmed from Mildred's respect and admiration for the elders as well as her sense of humour and fairness. For example, when Chief Amos Williams of Kitwancool (Gitanyow Band) said he could not sit for Mildred because he had to do the dishes, she grabbed a towel and began drying. He was surprised to have a white woman helping him with his chores. On another occasion, she helped a Sechelt man called Old Tom select a file at a hardware store, and then purchased it for him. She enjoyed seeing "his jaws… open like an old suitcase, then slowly a wide grin spread over his wrinkled face." After completing Tom's portrait, she gave him her lunch and paid for

Chucháwlut (Squamish)
1940, oil on board
24" x 18"
SQUAMISH NATION
COLLECTION
DAN FAIRCHILD PHOTOGRAPHY

Isaac Jacobs, 1943
oil on board, 20" x 16"
SQUAMISH NATION
COLLECTION
DAN FAIRCHILD PHOTOGRAPHY

his time. Mildred firmly believed that "old Indian people, as a rule, have so little that compensation should always be made in return for their goodwill." She thought it "grossly unfair" if other artists took advantage of the elders.[27]

Because Mildred lived in close proximity to the Squamish Nation, individuals from that community often rowed boats across Burrard Inlet and walked through Stanley Park to her home. Among the frequent visitors treated to tea and cake were Mathias Joe and Isaac Jacobs and his wife Lizzie. A Shaker minister, Isaac constructed a church in his backyard. He also built his own house, and in her unpublished writings, Mildred described him as a "man with unexampled industry." As Mildred wrote in *Potlatch People*, groups of "brother followers" from the United States or Vancouver Island would often come to Isaac's charmingly "most unorthodox church in a bleakly orthodox world." Often, Lizzie and Isaac would have to house the traveling faithful, their home becoming "an improvised hotel."[28] Isaac eventually erected a building that provided cooking, eating and sleeping quarters for his guests. The structure was also used to host special ceremonies and banquets.

In her unpublished writings, Mildred described how one afternoon, when Isaac and Lizzie were visiting, he mentioned how nice it would be to have a picture of Jesus for his church, "a dream" that Mildred realized "lay close to his heart." She noted his unspoken request and immediately "changed the subject. I didn't forget about it, however. The matter kept recurring to my mind. It bothered me, and finally I decided I had better go and find out just what it was that Isaac had in view." Taking her into the church, Isaac indicated "where he would like to see a picture of Jesus hanging behind the altar... a focal point for all to see.... He had not asked me to paint such a picture, but what he meant was clear as day."

Mildred explained to her friend that she had never before painted a religious portrait, but she would try. Isaac already had a frame, but when she returned home, Mildred discovered she "had a better frame than Isaac's of the right size, and a canvas to fit it. I gave the frame a fresh coat of paint and got busy on the painting."[29]

Mildred "felt unworthy even to... attempt" painting "the Master of Galilee." She was also unsure if she could

> fulfill the dreams of this humble and sincere Indian.... But Isaac had faith in me.... Gradually the painting evolved, the head in profile, with a strong light coming down from above as Isaac had visualized it.... Isaac's joy in having the painting more than compensated me for all my work, but he insisted on presenting me with a piece of his own carving to show his appreciation. "I have your work," he said, "now you have some of mine."[30]

A religious calendar in the Thornton family collection suggests Mildred used some of those images for reference. The finished work showed a European head with long hair and a beard (a common representation of Christ in the early twentieth century) looking heavenward with "broad, bands of warm, golden sunlight. His profile strongly outlined by the glowing rays." Mildred said, "I favor a more modern style of art, but this is not in the least modern."[31] Yet, she was pleased with the image and hoped the painting gave "the message of love and peace that Isaac cherished for his little sanctuary."[32] In the end, Isaac happily had his "Jesus Picture" for the Easter church services.

Mildred's portrait of Isaac conveys a, warm, intelligent, kindly minister in his robes. She emphasized his "big, solemn brown eyes," which she found "tender in contemplation."[33] Her study indicates an aura of distinction that was appropriate to a man who was the descendent of Pitsmek, a former chief noted for his leadership abilities.[34] Mildred's portraits indicate capable draftsmanship and a talent at conveying personality. Vanessa Campbell notes that, when comparing photographs of Squamish ancestors with Mildred's depictions, "they didn't have a lot of expression in the pictures; but, in the portraits they definitely have character.... [Mildred] tried to capture a certain moment or relationship she experienced with each individual."[35]

Art consultant Anthony Westbridge has settled numerous portraits with various First Nations for heritage programmes or archival projects. He says that, over the years, many band councils indicated an interest in acquiring their ancestors' portraits; unfortunately, not all had the funding to do so even though the sums were "modest." He also discovered, "Because of my contact with band councils, some family members also purchased paintings. Those individuals were keen to acquire the portraits: in most cases, they were the only extant images of the particular elders."

Westbridge vividly recalls a woman from the Bella Coola area who, for years, had been searching for the portrait of her grandfather. As a youngster, she had watched Mildred complete the study. Westbridge mailed the woman "images of various Band elders Thornton had painted. Ecstatic, she phoned to say that when she saw the image of her grandfather, she burst out crying. Needless to say, she acquired the painting."[36]

In the 1990s, the Squamish Nation, under the direction of Deborah Jacobs, the great-granddaughter of Isaac Jacobs, began collecting Mildred's portraits of their ancestors. Co-curated by Julie Baker and Janice George, and in conjunction with the West Vancouver Museum & Archives, the Squamish people exhibited fourteen of Mildred's portraits in Kw'achmixwáylh: Showing of the Pictures (the show ran from January 19 to August 29, 1999). Each painting was accompanied by a brief biography and, where possible, a photograph of the individual. The exhibition's objective was "a new one for museums" in that the Squamish community could

> share what is important to them, thereby providing the public with a bet-ter understanding of the history and values that they hold to be important. For example, when reading the biographies of the sitters in each portrait, the viewer gains a sense of the characteristics that are valued by the Squamish Nation—characteristics that are often not considered to be particularly central to European cultures.[37]

The portraits were also a catalyst to collecting information that contributed "to the recovery of an oral tradition, history and personal identity which had been in danger of being lost due to the past 100+ years of European influence."[38] Deborah Jacobs further describes the exhibition as "a sacred ceremony that celebrates and remembers the lives of the ones that have gone over to the other side."[39] At the exhi-bition's opening, Jack Thornton was invited to speak about his mother and several Squamish elders shared their recollections of Mildred.

Jacobs explains that she also "developed a fairly extensive educational program [based on the portraits] and introduced stories or narratives from the families on their ancestor."[40] Vanessa Campbell adds that the portraits are appreciated not "purely for art's sake. It is because of the representation of the ancestors, so it is the actual image that we value." She adds that the educational package is part of the Squamish education curriculum "that can be shared with current and future young

Deborah Jacobs,
Education Director,
Squamish Nation, in
Squamish Nation Chief
and Council Room
North Vancouver, 2010
DAN FAIRCHILD PHOTOGRAPHY

people."[41] One part of the programme has school children demonstrate and describe their connection to the images. The portraits are also part of a traveling education kit that has been shown at international conferences.

The portraits are positioned along a staircase, down a hallway and on into the Council Room of the Squamish Nation's administrative offices in North Vancouver. The community now has seventeen pictures and eventually hopes to own all twenty-four that Mildred painted. Her portraits remain highly regarded because "of their aspect of looking down on us, or watching over us, especially in the Chief and Council Room, which always reminds us where we come from."[42]

Another outcome from the Showing of the Pictures is that the public and institutions are more aware of the Squamish people's interest in repatriating artifacts. The exhibition "has triggered a lot of different things" for the community, including "other Thornton portraits being offered as well as early Squamish carvings and, in one case, ancestral remains being returned to the Nation."[43]

Mildred's work is also proving valuable in other ways. At some point, in addition to her paint box, boards and suitcase, she started packing a large and cumbersome

Red Crow (Kainai)
n. d., oil on board
20" x 15½"
THORNTON FAMILY
PRIVATE COLLECTION
PHOTO BY JANET DWYER

recording machine to document First Nations songs. She never sold the recordings, but did sometimes play the songs as part of her lectures. When Mildred was ill and nearing the end of her life, the B.C. Archives purchased the recordings. They can be listened to by researchers, but can only be reproduced with the permission of each pertinent First Nation. In at least two instances, the recordings have proven invaluable. In 1958, a representative from the Bella Coola Agency wrote Mildred asking for copies of songs she had recorded because "there is not enough of the old people left who remember the old songs."[44] Additionally, Mildred's 1956 recording of Nuxalk (Bella Coola) songs was "brought out" in 1997, becoming "valuable additions to the Nuxalk cultural canon because they provide access to songs and voices that have long been unheard or even forgotten." The song and movements for their Cedar Softening Dance/Bark Pounding had not been performed for many years. This ritual was

new to the living generations of Nuxalk who had never witnessed it. Its traditional family or individual owners had been forgotten…. The elders in the audience seemed joyful at seeing this new-old style song/dance brought out again. In this case, Western technology and anthropological sources [Mildred's recording] were… useful aids to cultural revival."[45]

Mildred's First Nations portraits are important historical records as well as artistic renderings. She was so determined to paint significant individuals that she painted a study of the already deceased Chief Red Crow from a newspaper photograph. Apparently, this was the only time she did not use a live model. Although once a famous warrior, Red Crow signed a treaty, settled on a reserve, led his people to self-sufficiency and encouraged education while retaining traditional customs and spiritual practices. Mildred obviously regarded him highly. Her portrait indicates a distinguished, peaceful, good-humoured countenance.

Mildred regarded her paintings as significant artifacts because the elders of the early twentieth century were the last to have lived traditional ways and could recall ancient ceremonies, legends and oral histories. In some cases, her depictions are the

only extant portrayals of certain individuals. Anthony Westbridge views Mildred's portrait collection "as one of the most important historical documents of the twentieth century in Canada, particularly as it relates to the First Nations."[46]

Unlike the stiff visages produced by early and lengthy photographic processes, Mildred's portraits convey personality and character. Mildred did not pose or stage her sitters; nor did she, like Paul Kane, select subjects that fit the romanticized and *imaginary* ideas of the North American Indian perpetuated in Western culture throughout the late nineteenth to the mid-twentieth century. Often, the individuals Mildred considered significant were elders: in honour of their years and their knowledge, she highlighted their wrinkles and age. She broke with portrait tradition in that she seldom painted hands; she rarely had the time. The majority of her work concentrates on heads and shoulders, presented in profile, frontal or three-quarter views that present a likeness as well as an artistically complex image. In a few cases, she employed objects, such as carvings or drums, to signify the artistic importance of an individual. Chief Jessea, Chief Herbert Johnson, Chief Mungo Martin and Chief Willie Seaweed are four examples of carvers who had samples of their work included in their portraits.

⌃ *Chief Moody Humchitt* (Heiltsuk), 1947, oil on board, 24" x 20"
ORIGINAL IN HEILTSUK NATION COLLECTION REPRODUCED FROM KODACHROME SLIDE IN THORNTON FAMILY PRIVATE COLLECTION, DIGITALLY RESTORED BY JANET DWYER

⌃⟨ *Chief Jessea* (Kitselas) n. d., oil on board 24" x 20"
PRIVATE COLLECTION DAN FAIRCHILD PHOTOGRAPHY

SIX

An Indomitable Spirit

Although he later described her as charming, gracious and dignified, when Reg Ashwell knocked on Mildred's door one evening in the autumn of 1962, he did not know what to expect. He was a forty-two-year-old entrepreneur and art collector (who later added author and founder of the Pegasus Gallery on Salt Spring Island to his credentials), and she was seventy-three. He had recently seen some of Mildred's work hanging in the Gallery of B.C. Arts. He thought they were "gorgeous,"[1] but the proprietor, Edith Clark, complained that the canvasses were too large for the gallery's crowded walls. Overhearing the conversation, Edith's husband, Herb, suggested that Reg and Mildred should meet. When they did, they became instant friends.

As soon as he entered Mildred's home, all Reg could see were paintings and aboriginal artwork. Walking into the hallway, he viewed a painting of the Fraser River: "The immensity of British Columbia and its brooding, lonely mountains, had been captured... right down to the muddy green of the Fraser's waters."[2] Captivated by the painting, Reg stumbled into a life-size Salish welcoming figure carved by

Mildred painting in her
Vancouver "studio"
1959
IB MEYER-OBEL PHOTOGRAPHER

First Nations art inside
Mildred Valley Thornton's
home 1959

IB MEYER-OBEL PHOTOGRAPHER

Mildred's late friend, Tommy Moses (Squamish Nation). On both sides of the door-way leading into the living room were two of Tommy's totem poles, approximately six feet in height.

Mildred described herself and Tommy as "Tillikums" (friends). One rainy day, Tommy arrived at her door, and after tea, she painted his portrait in the rare "comfort and convenience" of her studio. Mildred described Tommy as "a true artist" who liked "to carve for the same reason that I like to paint, which should be reason enough for anyone." She also stated that his carvings "all but breathe." Mildred obtained the tall totems because, in spite of ordering smaller ones, he had carved ones "twice as large and twice as much money as my order." However, she paid "without a whimper" because "you simply take what Tommy thinks is right for you and like it!"[3]

What Reg saw inside the house was "almost past accurate description." The kitchen was vibrant with green walls, red chairs and colourful pottery. Curtains in the living and dining-room were made of unbleached cotton decorated with vibrant bars of colour. There were "small totem poles, and other Indian carvings of every description… everywhere. They covered the window ledges and table tops, and the larger ones, including a fine Kwakiutl ceremonial paddle…, stood on the floor, or leaned against a wall." Along the mantelpiece was a collection of Inuit carvings. There were Haida drums, a Nuxalk moon mask (among others), Haida argillite carvings, Kwakwaka'wakw and Nuxalk spirit-bird masks and Nuu-chah-nulth baskets. There were also brightly coloured rugs with aboriginal themes that Mildred had hooked.[4]

On the stairs was a large Salish carving of a killer whale and an old Kwakwaka'wakw cedar bark mat. Upstairs Reg saw a blue ceremonial Kwakwaka'wakw blanket, a Haida red cedar killer whale headdress and a deerskin outfit once belonging to Pauline Johnson. Mildred explained that she had purchased or been given the artwork and regalia during her travels to various First Nations communities. The artifacts held personal significance for her as mementos of her trips and friendships, and as symbols of the respect in which many aboriginal people held her. Mildred viewed herself as an amateur ethnologist, preserving and protecting work she so highly regarded. She also showed Reg her large collection of books, mainly Canadiana: some poetry, but most of the shelves contained early writings on the First Nations of Canada.

"Obediah" on Mildred's front porch, 1959
IB MEYER-OBEL PHOTOGRAPHER

What mostly intrigued Reg, however, was "the color and vigor" of Mildred's work. He recalled that her paintings covered the walls of every room and stairwell, and filled the basement and a large attic room: "On one wall hung a large canvas painted in mauves and purples, showing a sunburst over the awesome mountains of Jervis Inlet, as they rise in almost perpendicular splendor from the quiet stillness of the water." Another was of the Similkameen Valley and there was one of Vaseux Lake in the B.C. Interior. Mildred told Reg, "B.C. is big…. No matter how you try, it never seems quite possible to really capture that impressive vastness on canvas."[5] That did not deter her from trying.

Reg recalled one "beautiful watercolor, depicting a stand of totem poles, which Mildred… had painted about twenty years previously at the ancient Tsimshian village of Kispiox, near Hazelton."[6] There were also many portraits, including one of Mary Capilano (1935), Mildred's first B.C. aboriginal portrait, and Mildred's old Cree friend Buffalo Bow (circa 1930). In addition, there were numerous paintings of First Nations villages.

After tea and cake, Mildred treated Reggie (as she always called him) by showing him her 35 mm kodachrome slides of B.C. peoples and communities.[7] Reg remembered:

Longhouse, Stanley Park
1945 (Squamish)
oil on board
dimensions unknown
PRIVATE COLLECTION
REPRODUCED FROM KODACHROME
SLIDE IN THORNTON FAMILY
PRIVATE COLLECTION, DIGITALLY
RESTORED BY JANET DWYER

Some of the villages, such as the Salish village that has disappeared from the Stanley Park area without a trace, Mildred carefully constructed on canvas from vivid accounts given her by very old native elders with long memories, such as the late chief August Jack (Khatsalano), who was born in Stanley Park.[8]

From 1962 to 1966, Reg and Mildred took day trips to various communities so she could paint. He also took her to several local First Nations dance festivals and gatherings. He recalls that Mildred would be so excited she would "scare the living daylights" out of him. As Reg was pulling up, "she would have the door open and her foot out. I was scared stiff she'd break a leg." Though he often reminded her not to do so, "She could never remember. She was always in a hurry."[9]

Many times Mildred ventured through isolated regions of Western Canada, often "to some remote Indian village, such as Kitwancool or Kispiox, to paint everything I saw there, whether it be a chief or a totem pole, that I felt should be recorded for posterity."[10] In addition, she regularly returned to the prairies, often visiting the Calgary Stampede, to record the Plains peoples and the grassland habitat.

As if trekking hundreds of miles through rugged country was not difficult enough, Mildred sometimes contended with ferocious storms and other dangerous or uncomfortable situations. In an unpublished story titled "Hazardous Journey," Mildred described a 1940s cruise up the coast to Skidegate. She said the *Cassiar* was "the world's narrowest ship, just about five good steps take you across her." The purser told her that the boat "had been condemned for years, that one of her boilers was cracked which made it unsafe for her to go faster than nine knots an hour—but she had always made the grade so far."

Most of the ship's passengers were loggers returning to camp "roaring drunk and dead broke after a few wild weeks in the city." Mildred described them as "unshaven,

unkempt, disheveled, and their language was more lurid than the flaming sunset."
The purser told Mildred that if the loggers became "too troublesome" they would be
put in the hold to sober up.

Mildred's cabin was "a tiny box… with two narrow bunks, and a miniature stool
in the corner. When I put my suitcase on the stool there wasn't room enough to open
it in comfort, so I performed this operation on the bunk." There was no key to lock
her door, only a "tiny bolt." Mildred "knew that one heave from the shoulders of a
husky logger would smash it like a paper box." She contemplated canceling the trip
but noted, "There is something in me that hates to admit defeat—something which
abhors turning back." When another woman joined her in the cabin, Mildred bol-
stered her courage with the idea that "two sober women ought to be able to handle
a whole shipload of drunk men." The ship sat at dock four hours past its sailing time.
The captain refused to let a "blind drunk" crew member board with "a huge case of
beer," and the rest of the crew would not work without the sailor. The crew member
and the beer were finally brought on board. Mildred and her cabin mate
decided to sleep fully clothed. Around one o'clock, the women "were just
getting settled… when there was a commotion immediately outside our
porthole. Someone was being violently ill by the railing." Mildred closed
the porthole, but the stuffy room soon caused her to reopen it.

Buffalo Bow (Cree)
circa 1930, oil on
canvas, 34" x 21"
THORNTON FAMILY
PRIVATE COLLECTION
PHOTO BY JANET DWYER

> At about three in the morning a man stuck his head in and bellowed, "Hello
> there sweethearts." When we didn't answer he kept repeating this endear-
> ing term, and there were smothered chuckles and whisperings outside.
>
> For a few moments all was silence—an ominous silence. Then someone
> knocked at our door.… Soon there was more knocking, scuffling, laugh-
> ing and rude jokes.… Wildly I wondered how I could defend myself, then
> groped around in the dark for the hat pin on the tam I had been wearing.
> Grimly clutching my primitive weapon, I muttered, "God help the first man
> who comes through the door. He will get it right up to the hilt.".… To my
> great relief the mob moved away, discouraged no doubt by our cold recep-
> tion. There was nothing worse than the ordinary hoodlumism during the
> remainder of the night, but needless to say there was no sleep for me.

The next night hangovers and stormy seas gave Mildred "malicious satisfac-
tion in the silence which enveloped the ship."

Mildred marveled at the isolation and beauty of each stop where "high mountains loomed, mysterious and foreboding through the mist and fog" and forests

> dark and defiant, marching down to the water's edge... [and] rich moist colors of rain on wood—red, brown, yellow, in contrast to the deep green of the trees. Only elemental things mattered here. Man, the intruder, was external, ephemeral and insignificant.[11]

While visiting Haida Gwaii, the famed Canadian ethnologist Marius Barbeau once invited Mildred on a proposed week-long trip to Langara Island. In her unpublished story "The Trip We Didn't Take," Mildred wrote, "There might be some totem poles—we might glean some information of historic value. That was reason enough for the professor to go, and reason enough for me." Once their ship, the *Western Hope*, left protected waters, they were hit by a ferocious storm. While the other passengers became ill and Mildred "was desperately frightened," Barbeau sat on deck "wedged comfortably in the little stairway at the stern... as undisturbed as though he were sitting in a church pew, to all intents and purposes blissfully unconscious of the roaring sea and his miserable companions." Instead of paintings, Mildred came away with an unforgettable experience and a new tale.

Mildred seems to have taken the ethnomusicologist Dr. Ida Halpern on one trip (possibly to Cape Mudge).[12] A Jewish émigré from Austria, from 1947 to sometime in the 1950s, she recorded over 500 songs from various B.C. aboriginal communities. They were made available to the public on Folkway Records albums with royalties going to the respective bands. Initially disparaged and jokingly nicknamed "Haida Ida," Halpern, like Mildred, persevered with her unconventional and self-appointed mission; as a result she preserved music of the Haida, Kwakwaka'wakw, Nuu-chah-nulth and other Coast Salish peoples. That legacy has been used for various documentaries and by the Kwakwaka'wakw U'Mista Cultural Society. Halpern also validated "the sophisticated and orderly complexity of Northwest Coast music."[13] Halpern shared one other interest with Mildred: both worked as Vancouver journalists. Halpern was the *Vancouver Province* music critic from 1952 to 1957.

Good humour, spunk and an adventurous spirit served Mildred well. As just one example (circa 1946), while she was visiting the Hazelton area, an RCMP officer and an Indian agent offered to take her along on their trip to remote Fort Babine. The manager of a Hazelton hotel loaned her a sleeping bag for the "crisp and frosty" nights. In the chilly mornings, Mildred relished the "fog… twining… like some ethereal scarf… around the throat of the mountain. A round, red benevolent sun" soon warming the autumn air. Mildred rejoiced in the "clean, sweet smell of pines" and the "keen, tonic air." She was overwhelmed by the rugged beauty that she found "will forever remain an incalculable repository of grandeur… to draw upon."[14]

Mildred described how they traveled by car to Topley Landing, and when offered a dinner of billy goat, Mildred said she would "try anything once" and found it "jolly good."

Untitled, n.d.
watercolour
REPRODUCED FROM KODACHROME
SLIDE IN THORNTON FAMILY
PRIVATE COLLECTION, DIGITALLY
RESTORED BY JANET DWYER

Untitled, n. d.
watercolour
REPRODUCED FROM KODACHROME
SLIDE IN THORNTON FAMILY
PRIVATE COLLECTION, DIGITALLY
RESTORED BY JANET DWYER

The rest of the trip was in an old leaky boat, with the men bailing approximately "120 gallons per hour." Despite worries regarding her safety, Mildred found herself in a "ravishing universe of abundance and diversity… apart from the world at war and of greed and competition." She began painting and noted, "I could see wonderful scenes approaching for quite some time before they passed and worked furiously to capture something of their fleeting glory." She did so for the entire day stressing, "What matter that I grew weary. Days like this were rare. Opportunities like this might never occur again. One scene after another I sketched in water colours, as they sped by." Each time she finished a sketch she showed it to her companions who cheered their appreciation. Mildred was so "thrilled and enthused," she went at it "fire and tongs" until they camped for the evening.[15]

The next day they arrived at Fort Babine where she had accommodation in a comfortable cabin. Mildred was so taken with the place, she enthused:

> As soon as I put my luggage down I sat on the back step and began making a sketch of the Indian village…. It was all so new to me and so vital I could hardly wait to record it. I could see an old woman scraping a large moose hide and a great deal of salmon hanging up to dry.

That painting captures the liveliness and vibrancy of the community, the sunshine "on the unpainted houses, turning the drab boards to a rich gold… the gaily clad" inhabitants and the "quilts and blankets of every imaginable hue"[16] hanging on the fences. The mood is so joyous that even the chimneys seem to be dancing.

During her visit, Mildred also attended a potlatch, which she enjoyed until the early morning hours. She did not believe that the ceremony should be outlawed, and she wrote newspaper articles in an attempt to educate the public to this injustice imposed upon B.C.'s First Nations.

On another occasion, while she was visiting the residential school at Kakawis on the rugged west coast of Vancouver Island, Mildred set out by dugout canoe to locate Chief Napoleon Maquinna. When Mildred and her paddler, Brother MacDonald, met Chief Maquinna on a fishing boat, Napoleon transferred to the canoe. As Brother MacDonald was rowing into shore, a big wave slapped Mildred "in the back with a tremendous wallop as a tumultuous white wall of water broke over me like a miniature Niagara, soaking me thoroughly from the waist down." Because she had so much to carry, "five parcels for one pair of hands," Mildred had not packed much clothing. She had just recovered from a bout of pneumonia, and she did not want to stay in wet attire. With her palette knife, she cut off the drenched section of her vest, but her girdle was also saturated. Grabbing her paint rags, she stuffed them between her girdle and her back. After hanging her wet clothing to dry, changing her shoes and socks, and putting on her only other dress, Mildred had "fun painting Chief Maquinna." Afterwards, the priest invited Mildred to speak to the boys attending the residential school. As she was giving the students an art lesson, she "suddenly... felt something slip. Horrors! My paint rags had come loose from their moorings."

Indian Village Near Fort Babine (Wit'at)
circa 1943, oil on board
30" x 40"
PRIVATE COLLECTION
DAN FAIRCHILD PHOTOGRAPHY

She managed to move to the back of the room while engaging "the children in rapid fire conversation, [and] giving them directions for intense application to work. Safely in the corner, I managed to hitch myself together well enough to finish the lesson." Undaunted, once changed she "heaved a vast sigh of relief" for she had attained her goal of painting Chief Maquinna and "pleased the children and avoided a cold."[17] She had also learned that packing a change of clothes was highly important.

For years, Mildred had wanted to paint Sarah Gunanoot, the wife of the famous renegade Simon Gunanoot, as she viewed both of them as significant characters in First Nations history. After repeatedly missing Sarah, Mildred heard from the Hazelton Indian agent that Sarah was at the Cassiar Cannery. Mildred was in Prince Rupert and travelled to Port Edward where she caught a fish packer to Cassiar. Sarah "grinned happily from ear to ear" when Mildred asked to paint her portrait. They went to a net loft where Sarah sat on a pile of netting. Mildred found that Sarah's "face took on something of the sadness and sorrow she had known [for] so many years." Mildred saw the hardships "written on the face of Old Sarah as she sat there pensively in the net loft." Arriving late back at Port Edward, Mildred managed to catch a ride back to Prince Rupert "triumphant" with her "treasured canvas" tucked

Sarah Gunanoot
(Tsimshian), 1948
oil on board, 24" x 20"
REPRODUCED FROM KODACHROME
SLIDE IN THORNTON FAMILY
PRIVATE COLLECTION, DIGITALLY
RESTORED BY JANET DWYER

"under my arm."[18] Sarah's portrait is unusual for its background of fishing nets. Simple curtains of colour framed most of Mildred's First Nations sitters; sometimes background carvings highlighted that the individual was an artist. In this case, the netting seems to symbolize the web of poverty, racism and adversity that had ensnared Sarah's life.

No matter how many supplies Mildred carted on her expeditions, she often ran short or was unprepared when she found a subject. During those times, she painted on whatever material she could find. Portraits in her collection are on art board, plywood, Masonite, cardboard and even discarded doors. On one occasion, she packed only a couple of brushes and a few used paint tubes because she was embarking on a lecture tour of the Okanagan. When leaving for her trip, she had commented to her husband, "Who knows… I may catch up to Big William at last." He was the chief of the Salmon Arm Reserve, and she had missed meeting him a couple of times. She was successful on that trip, but she had neither boards nor a palette. The hotel manager gave her a discarded door. The local druggist had no linseed oil, but he gave her a bottle, which was filled for no charge at the local hardware store. Mildred then traveled to the chief's home, only to realize that she did not have a palette on which to mix her paints. Big William's wife solved the problem by providing Mildred with a dinner plate, thus ending that trip's "programme of improvisation."[19]

Mildred's zeal was never extinguished, no matter how arduous the task. When she met Mrs. Long Time Squirrel, from the Kainai (Blood) Nation in Alberta, the old woman was helping to erect a Holy Woman's Lodge. She was not going to interrupt her activity to pose, so Mildred ran back and forth... sketching like fury, exerting every ounce of energy and skill of which I was capable whilst I clung to my equipment.... I was able to get a recognizable likeness of the agile old lady which I shall always treasure."[20]

While she stressed that she did not rework or retouch portraits once back in her studio, there is evidence to suggest otherwise. On a few occasions, Mildred seems to have wanted to add detail or perhaps improve a study. As a result, there are two versions of a few portraits, including Chief Manitouwassis, Mary Capilano, Chief Ben Pasqua and Chief Jimmy John.

Princess Louisa Inlet/ Jervis Inlet, n.d.
oil on canvas
26½" x 37¼"
PRIVATE COLLECTION
DAN FAIRCHILD PHOTOGRAPHY

Mildred considered her documentation of aboriginal people as following in the footsteps of the Canadian painter Paul Kane. Unlike his, Mildred's paintings were not an attempt to propagate a non-aboriginal perspective. She was trying to work as a witness: preserving for history the images of people who had lived traditional lifestyles, especially the elders who were the repositories of aboriginal history prior to the upheaval and destruction of their communities brought on by non-aboriginals. She was ahead of her time in the celebration of the elderly and of marginalized people. She wanted her portraits and depictions of early First Nations ceremonies to perpetuate new and respectful views of our country's indigenous inhabitants. Others, like B.C.'s Patricia Richardson Logie (born in 1925) and James Houston (1921–1995, OC, FRSA, and an advocate of Inuit art and culture during the 1950s and 1960s) have followed in her footsteps, but Mildred's work is unequalled.[21] Her paintings are artistically distinctive, a form of social advocacy; indeed, her advocacy can be viewed as a form of quiet activism. As one journalist suggested in 1961, "increasing interest... [in B.C.] and abroad in Indian art and... culture" was due to the years Mildred "spent... fostering interest in... Indian heritage and a lifetime of painting portraits."[22]

A Gutsy Artist

Besides her portrayals of aboriginal people and their customs, Mildred never tired of recording her impressions of B.C.'s diverse landscapes. She usually made small sketches in watercolour and, after returning home, would repaint the vistas in larger watercolour formats or in oils. She remarked that one month of travel would result in six months of studio work. Her simple but dramatic compositions and her usually deliberate brushstrokes were modernist in style. She admitted that her palette choices were often more vibrant than that of the actual scene, but she used colour as a means to convey the ruggedness, immensity or majestic aspects of the landscape. As with her oil paintings, Mildred's watercolour studies are energetic and engaging. The viewer feels the ruggedness of mountain terrain, the sun-dappled seclusion of a forest, a lazy-flowing northern river, the turbulence of a rocky stream or the mystical watchfulness of secluded totem poles.

Ian Sigvaldason, of Pegasus Gallery of Canadian Art on Salt Spring Island, first encountered Mildred's work a few years ago. He notes that Mildred had such a different voice from the famous West Coast painters at the time: Emily Carr, Lawren Harris, Jock MacDonald, B.C. Binning, E.J. Hughes and W.P. Weston…. The oils were extremely confident and passionate, and I found the watercolours very loose, vibrant and exciting…. She used purples, blues, oranges and colours that people typically and traditionally wouldn't have used in their watercolours, especially in the '30s, '40s and '50s… My response to her paintings is the same as my clients': as soon as you see her work, you can't unring that bell. Most of the clients who contact me never have an interest in selling Mildred's work. The paintings have been in the family for a generation or two…. The fact that she was ostracized by some in the arts community, and that maybe some of her work was not considered historically or even politically correct, no longer matters.[1]

From her earliest exhibitions, collectors have responded to Mildred's work. One family has twenty-three Thornton watercolours hanging on a bedroom wall (and

Untitled, n.d.
watercolour
8½" x 11¼"
THORNTON FAMILY
PRIVATE COLLECTION
PHOTO BY JANET DWYER

six more elsewhere in the house). The husband bought the first one and, over the years, has continued to surprise his wife on her birthdays, anniversaries or other special occasions with Thornton paintings. She says her husband "feels very lucky to find any of Mildred's watercolours…. My husband and daughter each have one of Mildred's oil paintings, but I prefer her watercolours." Most are small and have been hung in groupings: boat studies, Fraser River scenes, Stanley Park, totem poles, historic studies like old sawmills and Vancouver landscapes: The couple like to view the work upon waking:

> You look at them, and ten minutes later you see something you didn't see the first time. It is also fun to wonder, Where was Mildred when she painted this? One painting is of the Benson Shipyards in Vancouver. We used to go and fish shiners off those docks, years ago…. You don't see that anymore…. You have to give Mildred credit for doing what she did in those days. It was pretty tremendous.[2]

Brockton Point, Stanley Park, n.d., watercolour
6" x 8"
PRIVATE COLLECTION

As with her oil studies, Mildred favoured purples, pinks, greens and blues in her watercolour paintings. Her palette did change from time to time as she experimented or was affected by her surroundings or other artists. Drawn as she was to Canadian and agrarian iconography, the modernist depictions of the city's concrete grain elevators by the well-known photographer John Vanderpant attracted Mildred's attention. Although industrial images were uncommon subjects for her, Mildred painted several depictions of the concrete towers (in both watercolours and oils). One small untitled painting is reminiscent of Vanderpant's studies, in that she painted a close-up view of only the upper portions of the structures, thereby putting them somewhat out of context. As well, her interplay of lines, forms, shadows and light was also a feature of Vanderpant's work. While only 5 1/8 by 8 3/8 inches, the watercolour conveys the monumentality of the cylindrical storage facility. Like Vanderpant's interpretations, Mildred's study portrays the "strength of form and cement—the tenderness… of texture—[and] the design possibility in form and shadow relationship."[3]

Vanderpant shared Mildred's nationalism, and both were committed to the development of Canadian art. They shared the belief that artists had a "duty" to present new ideas and perspectives, and to "express a national beauty."[4] When Mildred settled in Vancouver in the mid-1930s, Vanderpant was a vital cultural influence in the city. While earning his living as a talented portrait photographer,

he was also noted internationally for his modernist prints of plants, vegetables and concrete grain elevators. Vanderpant glorified his images with titles such as *Temples by the Seashore* and *Colonnades of Commerce*. In her large oil canvas *Temples of Commerce*, Mildred's title pays direct homage to her friend and his ideas on the dramatic and symbolic significance of the silos. Stylistically, however, Mildred's interpretation is distinctively hers. Vanderpant's grain elevators were mostly devoid of people and human-related elements (cars, houses, street lights and telephone poles were sometimes evident) and were often close-up views without external contexts. In

~ *SS Haro*, n. d., watercolour
5¾" x 8¼"
PRIVATE COLLECTION
DAN FAIRCHILD PHOTOGRAPHY

⌃ *Ships at Dock, New Westminster, BC*
n. d., watercolour, 13½" x 10"
PRIVATE COLLECTION
DAN FAIRCHILD PHOTOGRAPHY

⌃ *Boats, Benson Shipyards*
n. d. watercolour, 5¾" x 8⅜"
PRIVATE COLLECTION
DAN FAIRCHILD PHOTOGRAPHY

Mildred's painting, the imposing cathedral-like edifice dominates the foreground while being framed by the natural elements of sky, mountains and ground vegetation. The severity of the lines is accentuated by the cool tones that stress the grandeur and authority of the industrial shrine.

Another image that is similar to one of Vanderpant's prints is Mildred's study *After the Forest Fire*. She may have seen *In the Wake of the Forest Fire* (1926) at Vanderpant's studio or in one of his many illustrated lectures. Mildred once saw a fire-decimated locale where "stark, tall, blackened and ghostly the naked skeletons of… trees stabbed the bright, blue sky."[5] While she tended to paint more lush or majestic mountain and forest scenes, Vanderpant's study (reminiscent of work by the Group of Seven), may have inspired her to paint what would not traditionally have been considered an enticing landscape. Like Vanderpant, she chose to portray a dramatic representation of an atypical vision of beauty so as to evoke an emotional response.

A spiritual individual who believed that "art is the echo of the absolute,"[6] Vanderpant may have influenced Mildred's interest in the metaphysical. At the time, interest in theosophy, Christian Science and other spiritualistic beliefs was rampant across the country and intriguing to many artists. While his parents did sometimes attend the United Church, Jack Thornton says they "were never particularly religious." For a couple of years in the 1930s, however, his mother

≈ *Grain Elevators,* n. d.
watercolour, 5⅛" x 8⅜"
PRIVATE COLLECTION
DAN FAIRCHILD PHOTOGRAPHY

⌃ *Temples of Commerce,* n. d.
oil on canvas, 30" x 24"
PRIVATE COLLECTION
DAN FAIRCHILD PHOTOGRAPHY

became interested in something called the Metaphysical Society. I remember they met Sunday evenings in the old Georgia Hotel. They didn't have a church, so they had a… room… they met in. It was a full congregation with a Sunday school…. My brother and I… were completely bemused by the whole thing. When I was older, I recall thinking, "What a weird bloody lot that was!" How on Earth did my mother ever become interested in something like that? My old dad would just go along with anything she wanted: but, someone or something must have had an influence on her.

Sometimes, Mildred used watercolours for the effects she wanted; other times, her reasons were more practical. If she was traveling in search of aboriginal portraits, she wanted to save her boards for those studies. Watercolours could be executed quickly, dried on the spot and were easier to transport. Often, she would sketch a landscape in watercolour and repaint the image in oils in her studio. Occasionally, she seems

After the Forest Fire
n. d., oil on board
24" x 30"
PRIVATE COLLECTION
DAN FAIRCHILD PHOTOGRAPHY

to have worked a scene in both mediums, playing with the differences that could be achieved in each. One example is her painting *The Hao Hao Dance of the Bella Coolas* (1947). The watercolour is an impressive work, and it is deemed "terrific" by the internationally renowned B. C. artist Gordon Smith.[7] Disembodied masks seem to come alive as they stare out from a dark, mysterious background. The flowing lines of hot red ruffs emanating from the masks highlight the hypnotic aspects of the looming birds that seem to be speaking to the viewer. The masks have a supernatural presence, drawing the viewer into the circular pattern but also restricting entrance with large, penetrating eyes. The hypnotic image conveys a sacred and secret cultural tradition. Both the watercolour, which she likely executed during the dance, and the oil painting are vigorous with movement and deep pigments. The version she preserved on slide pulses with colour and action but is less abstract in that the legs and bodies of the dancers and the background are more clearly visible.

Like Emily Carr and many others (including Unity Bainbridge, Edwin Holgate, Langdon Kihn, A.Y. Jackson, W.J. Phillips and Ann Savage), Mildred traveled to remote First Nations communities to paint totem poles, villages and scenes of daily life. Mildred always sketched or painted totem poles on site. She did not paint anywhere near the number completed by Carr (approximately two hundred), but Mildred's interpretations (approximately forty) have their own distinctive style. For example, *Weeping Totem at Tanu* is painted in gray-blues and greens. Leaning into a background thicket topped by an expanse of cloud and sky, the solitary pole is striking for its isolation and melancholy. *The Crying Totem* by Emily Carr, a painting of the same pole, indicates a much more preternatural interpretation.

The Hao Hao Dance of the Bella Coolas, circa 1947 watercolour
15" x 20"
PRIVATE COLLECTION
DAN FAIRCHILD PHOTOGRAPH

The Hao Hao Dance of the Bella Coolas, circa 1947, oil on canvas
30" x 40", REPRODUCED FROM KODACHROME SLIDE IN THORNTON FAMILY PRIVATE COLLECTION, DIGITALLY RESTORED BY JANET DWYER

Cape Mudge, n. d.
watercolour
10½" x 13¾"
PRIVATE COLLECTION
DAN FAIRCHILD PHOTOGRAPHY

Even though the work and stories of Mildred and Carr differ vastly, there are comparisons and contrasts worth highlighting. Both artists were influenced by the intense palettes of the Fauvists, but Carr eventually came to employ expressionist, and sometimes cubist, influences in her work. Carr's major motifs were totem poles and trees and forests that convey sensual, brooding, rhythmic and mysterious qualities based on her sense of the divine. Mildred's landscapes never focused on one symbol, and her vision of Canada's wild terrain was conveyed through energetic brushstrokes and jubilant colour. Finally, an outgoing individual, Mildred rejoiced in painting people, whereas the more introverted Carr said, "I hate painting portraits." She only completed a few because she was "embarrassed" at the "impertinence and presumption" of exposing a sitter's character, and Carr thought the intense interaction between painter and model made the sitter feel "indecent and naked."[8]

Both women were passionate about aboriginal culture. But while Carr's paintings are romantic and imbued with elegiac feelings for what she thought was a disappearing race, Mildred's realistically focus on the historical and cultural significance of aboriginal life. Carr painted totem poles mainly as manifestations of the spirit world in nature; Mildred, on the other hand, painted a broad range of First Nations activities (approximately fifty) including potlatches, special ceremonies, folklore and work-related activities such as fishing.

The two also had literary interests. Mildred was an amateur poet, an art critic for the *Vancouver Sun*, a freelance journalist and an award-winning author (Canadian Authors' Association, 1966). Carr wrote several books; her first, *Klee Wyck* (1941), won a Governor General's Award. Both had engaging literary styles that were marked by humour and vivid descriptions. In addition, each became nationally acclaimed, with Mildred being described "as Canadian as hard wheat."[9]

Weeping Totem at Tanu
n. d., watercolour
14 ½" x 10½"
PRIVATE COLLECTION
PHOTO BY JANET DWYER

Mildred was dismayed that some individuals thought she was copying Carr, especially as she considered Carr's work too dark and somber. According to Mildred's son Jack, being compared to Carr "used to get right up my mother's hooter because she thought Emily Carr should be compared to her, not the other way around."

Carr and Mildred did not like one another, and their personal animosities may have stemmed from a sense of rivalry. They were vying for recognition in a sphere dominated by men. As well, unlike many of their female counterparts, they were not "sympathetic to themes that reaffirm and dramatize the importance of life—painting children, young women, and mothers and children."[10] Gordon Smith adds that Mildred's work

> wasn't like a woman's [of the era]: by that I mean she did not make pretty pictures. She was gutsy. Her work reminds me a little of the freshness of Tom Thomson's. She was really, really good. I hope she gets some recognition now.[11]

Mildred's work was often described as robust or masculine. Her response was, "I paint things as I see them, and

Three Tall Totems, n. d.
oil on board, 14" x 11"
PRIVATE COLLECTION
JOHN CAMERON PHOTOGRAPHY

there is nothing particularly effeminate about the Canadian landscape."[12] She emphasized that Canada is "not a 'pretty' country," but one that is "tremendous, magnificent, [and] over-powering."[13]

After World War I, female artists began garnering more recognition, but not "the attention their work warranted."[14] Indeed, the work of Canada's early female artists is only beginning to receive serious consideration. Unfortunately, the two most talented and independent female B.C. painters of the day never collaborated or celebrated their achievements; instead, they were forced to compete with one another.

Mildred's review of Carr's last exhibition at the Vancouver Art Gallery in 1943 is indicative of her insightful and forthright nature. She wrote:

> There is something courageous and remarkable in the spectacle of this woman no longer young and in very poor health, painting with such profusion and with growing power at an age when many are laying down their tools and slackening in their mental concepts.

Mildred described one canvas, *Light Swooping Through,* as "outstanding" and "full of the lush, throbbing life of the forest" and *Cedar* as "spectacular." She also bitingly stated that Carr was not "versatile" but "definitely an individual."[15] Carr was disappointed with the Vancouver reviews of her exhibition and stated in a prickly response to her friend Ira Dilworth: "I'd love to tip Delisle [Parker of the *Province*] and Valley Thornton out of a boat into [a] neck deep mud-puddle."[16] After Carr's death, Mildred wrote a review that would have appeased the solitary painter. She called her a "great artist," who made a "monumental effort" and who "saw keenly and deeply, and was able to record those impressions with unusual power.... Carr's natural reverence for all essential and primeval things enabled her to see it accurately and to record it with truth and feeling."[17] Sadly, these two extraordinary women never had a chance to sit down at Mildred's table to savour a cup of tea and a slice of cake.

Mildred's *Three Tall Totems* and *The Sentinel* exemplify the contrast between her style and Carr's. Both paintings reflect an impressionist style. In the former, the totems reverberate and shimmer with an august and enchanting grandeur. The detail on the poles is unclear, imbuing them with an ethereal quality that is enhanced by the high-keyed tones and paint textures: parts of the carvings seem to be transforming into animate forms. In the latter, the interaction between the human and the mystical is emphasized, and the differences between them are indistinguishable.

Mildred's interest in aboriginal life was enhanced by her belief that "native culture… [had] no counterpart in all the world." She was deeply drawn to aboriginal art for she viewed First Nations as "socially conscious people who produced art… for its own sake yet art which had something to say, positively and sincerely." Mildred also appreciated that aboriginal "artists were highly regarded. Only they could produce in enduring form for all the world to see proof of prestige and power as displayed in the great totem poles." Mildred regarded indigenous carvings as a "living form" and "history recorded in wood," the product of a "virile, exuberant, and resourceful people who were part of all they produced and [who] passed it [their art] on to future generations as a proud and unique heritage."[18]

The Sentinel, n. d.
oil on board, 10" x 12"
PRIVATE COLLECTION
JOHN CAMERON PHOTOGRAPHY

Mildred's friendships with a number of aboriginal elders gave her access to sacred and secret ceremonies. Privileged to hear stories and myths of several tribes, Mildred was fascinated with and revered the various cultures she encountered, which only furthered her desire to document and preserve them as historical records. She became an amateur ethnologist, recording stories, songs and observations; in addition, she painted dances and rituals she observed. *Mask Dance of the Bella Coolas* (circa 1943) is one striking example. Uno Langmann considers that work to be "a great painting."[19] The image is intriguing for its use of contrasts: humans as compared to supernatural beings; masked versus unmasked faces; the age and youth of the two

Mask Dance of the Bella Coolas, circa 1943
oil on board, 30" x 40"
REPRODUCED FROM KODACHROME
SLIDE IN THORNTON FAMILY
PRIVATE COLLECTION, DIGITALLY
RESTORED BY JANET DWYER

dancers; the exposed body and upper limbs of the child as compared to the undisclosed physical presence of the adult; the differing visages and heights of the masked observers; and the predominance of red and green, complements across the colour wheel. Moreover, while two of the dancers seem immersed in and entranced by the ritual, the others stare wonderingly and guardedly at them and the audience/viewer. The overall effect is that of a powerful secret ceremony.

Mildred also painted images from tales she heard. In 1965, Wilson Duff (Curator of Anthropology, Provincial Museum) criticized those depictions as not being historically accurate;[20] they are, nonetheless, dynamic interpretations. One such painting, *Hunting Whale,* highlights the strength and courage of the Northwest Coast aboriginals. The fishers strenuously paddle through turbulent waves towards a large whale as the animal seems to be menacingly turning toward them. The mood is dramatic and mythical.

Kwakwaka'wakw Initiation Ceremony (also titled *Warrior Dance)*, circa 1945
oil on board, 30" x 40"
PRIVATE COLLECTION
DAN FAIRCHILD PHOTOGRAPHY

Based on descriptions from Kwakwaka'wakw elders of a coming-of-age ceremony, *Kwakwaka'wakw Initiation Ceremony* (circa 1945, also known as *Warrior Dance*), is another powerful depiction. Like the Sun Dance of the Plains Indians and the potlatches in B.C., this initiation ceremony was outlawed because of its perceived brutality. Rather than seeming cruel, Mildred's image conveys the mystical aspects of the ritual. The carved totem and the masked figure in the foreground reinforce the spiritual significance of the event. They, along with the man with crossed arms who is leaning against the back wall, look towards the viewer as if barring outsiders from (or criticism of) the transformative event; as well, the regalia of the onlookers, the naked men and the disembodied arms raising the warrior convey a deeply rooted cultural and ritualistic dimension. According to the owners of this painting, what especially arrests viewers is the way the aboriginal initiate is suspended by ropes at the centre of the work in a fashion that suggests Christ on the cross, an effect that references two cultures—the subject's and the painter's.

While Mildred's depictions of aboriginal life and culture may not be completely "pure" or accurate, they are respectful and spirited. She presented the ceremonies and rituals as a form of enlightenment that would help transcend cultural differences and barriers. Those paintings are an extraordinary contribution to Canadian art history and the First Nations peoples of Western Canada.

Hunting Whale, n. d.
oil on board, 30" x 40"
PRIVATE COLLECTION
REPRODUCED FROM BUTLER
GALLERIES CATALOGUE

EIGHT

A Big Statement

I n 1969, Uno Langmann became a partner in Dr. Laurie Patrick's company, The Tappit Hen Limited, selling art and antiques. As was characteristic of Mildred's life, Patrick was her friend as well as her physician. Patrick's daughter, Jo Rappaport, says he was "irate" that no institution purchased Mildred's collection before or after her death: "He thought she was an original character and an artist who was given short shrift."[1] After Mildred's death, Langmann and Patrick were the first to buy paintings from her estate. Langmann remembers that Jack Thornton was "quite reluctant to break up the collection, but what else could have been done?"[2] Langmann and Patrick bought seven of the portraits reproduced in *Indian Lives and Legends*. When the two dissolved their partnership in 1971, they flipped a coin for first choice of the paintings not yet sold. Langmann won and chose what he thought was the best, *Siyámlut* (*Siamelaht, "Aunt Polly"*). The other portrait he selected was *Chief Herbert Johnson*.

Periodically, Langmann found paintings by Mildred in auctions and says he "always bid on them." He describes Mildred as "a very competent painter," adding:

⟨ *Whytecliff,* circa 1950s
30" x 36"
THORNTON FAMILY
PRIVATE COLLECTION
PHOTO BY JANET DWYER

There are very few people who can paint in watercolours and oils. There are very few people who can span landscape and go into portraiture…. [Mildred was accomplished in both mediums and subjects.] Her work is full of life. She had a wonderful palette, which you do not see with many other painters. There is cheerfulness to her work and immediacy in her paintings.[3]

Langmann thinks Mildred's landscapes are "wonderful," and he describes *B.C. Coastal Scene, Mountains and Sea* (circa 1948) as "a very strong painting." However, he does not think Mildred's landscapes have

the same depth of feeling as her portraits. Many of the early female painters used very light, pastel colours: Statira Frame, Mary Ritter Hamilton, Sophie Pemberton—they used a lot of pink and mauves. Mildred, and Emily Carr, turned to stronger colours. I think Mildred's landscapes helped her to develop strength in her palette. She used pure colour, almost straight from the tube, and she was one of the first female Canadian painters to do so.

At the time, nobody painted the volume of portraits that Mildred did, and nobody painted portraits better than Mildred did, including Emily Carr. What strikes me about Mildred's work is its power. I didn't know the sitters, but I can feel Mildred's desire to demonstrate the character and history of the people she depicted. She used strong colours because she wanted to emphasize the strength of the aboriginal people. She used her ability to convey the spirits of her sitters… Mildred made a big statement… I would love to have met her.[4]

After having his mother's estate appraised by Torben Kristiansen, owner of the Art Emporium in Vancouver, Jack Thornton and Kristiansen struck a deal. Reg Ashwell recalls Kristiansen saying, "Mildred stood firmly on her own two feet as a great Canadian artist in her own right."[5] For several years, the Art Emporium sold her work for Mildred's heirs. Collectors were keen to purchase the paintings, but the curators of civic galleries, archives and museums showed little interest. Then Kristiansen and Jack had a falling out. In 1985, with a home crammed with "four or five hundred paintings," Jack contacted Anthony Westbridge, of Westbridge Fine Art, who has represented Mildred's estate ever since. He was familiar with Mildred's paintings, having seen some at the Gallery of B.C. Arts. The proprietor of that business, Edith Clark, was a friend of Mildred's and a proponent of her work. Advertisements in the local newspapers indicate that Clark sold Thornton watercolours for many years after Mildred's death.

The first thing Westbridge did with Mildred's estate was hold a large exhibition and sale of ninety paintings in conjunction with Butler Galleries (November 16 to December 8, 1985). Having newly relocated in downtown Vancouver, Butler Galleries was spacious, with approximately 3,500 square feet. Co-owner Alison Bridger remembers:

> We had eighteen-foot ceilings with Gyproc walls, so the gallery was a perfect hanging space for such an extensive show. We were a rare and antiquarian book, map and print gallery, with one of the first cappuccino bars in the city, so having a kitchen meant we had the facility to put on a proper exhibition with food and drink. Our openings were always big parties, and there was a huge turnout for the Thornton retrospective, including the press. There were a great many portraits and both large and small landscapes in oil and watercolour. The show sold very well.
>
> At the time, the curators at the Vancouver Art Gallery seemed to have quite a dismissive attitude towards Mildred's work. They seemed to have the notion that it was simply derivative of the Group of Seven, and I think that's why her reputation had languished; however, at the gallery we recognized her paintings as being part of that larger continuum. The Native portraits are distinctive: she really captured the character of each individual, her use of colour was fabulous, her composition excellent and her very best work phenomenal. Part of her appeal to us was that there was absolutely no bullshit about her, and it showed in her paintings. This exhibit was an eye-opener for a lot of people.[6]

The Snow Beyond, n.d.
oil on canvas, 12½" x 10"
PRIVATE COLLECTION
DAN FAIRCHILD PHOTOGRAPHY

Stephen Lunsford, the rare-book dealer who shared space with Butler Galleries, wrote the text for the exhibition catalogue, which also included a short memoir by Jack Thornton, "My Mother 'Owas-ka-[ta]-esk-ean': A Personal Tribute." Published by Westbridge and Lunsford, the fifty-page catalogue, now a collector's item, is beautifully illustrated with colour and black-and-white plates.

Anthony Westbridge says:

> I know collectors that have many of Mildred's pieces, fabulous collections, and they won't let them go. In 1985, a woman bought one of Mildred's landscapes at

the Butler Galleries' exhibition. A few years later, I phoned the woman because I had a client who really wanted that painting. He was willing to pay double what the woman had paid. She said, "I desperately need money. You can come over to my house and take anything else you want, but you are not getting that painting." I could have put several thousand dollars into her pocket, but she would not part with Mildred's painting. While I haven't had another story as dramatic as that one, I have had several other people say, "You can take anything, but you can't have my Thornton." It's just amazing.

I have seen some spectacular Thornton paintings over the past twenty-five years. I think Mildred had the uncanny knack of capturing the real essence of the person who sat for her. The reason I say that is I have shown these portraits to family members and, without me saying anything, the families have known whom the painting was of. One day, Narcissus Blood, from the Blood Band Council, came to my gallery. I had about eighteen Blood portraits lined up against the wall. Without me telling him who they were, he immediately identified nearly every one…. Mildred looked at a person, and she knew the most important point to emphasize. That in itself is magnificent. She made no attempt whatsoever to beautify. If a guy had a cabbage nose and a cauliflower ear, that's what she gave him because that's who he was.

Then there is Mildred's painterliness: her faces are like landscapes. When I look at the brushstrokes, I think of that quote [in a Seattle newspaper], "No woman has the right to paint with so much power."[7] She painted people's faces with such energy and boldness as if she were painting a vibrant landscape. It's exciting just to look at the brushwork. Then you add to that the fact that in some cases she had such a short while to capture the individual—that is why she is so special.

I think Mildred is the second most important early female artist in B.C. Indeed, along with Emily Carr and certain members of the Beaver Hall Hill Group and the Emma Lake School, she has to be in the top echelon of all Canadian women artists…. She spent her entire life doing something that is historically and culturally important. And it wasn't just her art. Besides being a brilliant and versatile painter, she contributed through books and newspaper articles, lectures, seminars and critiques.

During the 1940s, Mildred's paintings and art reviews were well-received by local artists, the art community and the public. She wrote about significant and lesser exhibitions and artists, offering support and encouragement whenever possible. Unity Bainbridge (Order of British Columbia) graduated from the Vancouver School of Art in 1936 and strove for recognition for many years. She says she never had any money, so "it was always struggle, struggle." Unity appreciated Mildred's reviews: "She was kind to me and gave me lots of encouragement, which is darn well what we all needed. She was great."[8]

Mildred's assessments were valued by many, as is evidenced by the letters of thanks she received from both amateur and professional artists. In 1944, B.C. Binning stated, "You were both sensitive & understanding to what I am trying to do—& you said it clearly. May I be the critic now & say, 'Good Journalism.'" That same year, a lesser known painter, Alyce Shearer, wrote Mildred to thank her for the encouragement because "aspirants" such as Shearer had "an up-hill grade to climb in this city." Another artist, Jack G. Nilan, thanked Mildred for her "good stiff criticism... deserved... but you took a nice friendly attitude for which I... express deep appreciation."[9]

The Vancouver Art Gallery (VAG) opened in 1931, but for several ensuing decades, the arts community suffered tempestuous growing pains, "turmoil and heated arguments."[10] Many of those appeared in the local newspapers as letters to the editor. In

Old Blind Helen (Cree)
1942, oil on board
24" x 18", REPRODUCED
FROM KODACHROME SLIDE
IN THORNTON FAMILY
COLLECTION, DIGITALLY
RESTORED BY JANET DWYER

Stanley Como (Ktunaxa)
1948, oil on board
24" x 18"
PRIVATE COLLECTION
DAN FAIRCHILD PHOTOGRAPHY

1939, G. Van Houghten complained about the quality of art criticism, as well as the work of the VAG's hanging committee whom Van Houghten described as having "no knowledge of what constitutes art."[11] The city's early art critics provided more personal comments about the artists than critical comments on their work. In 1938, J. Delisle Parker, who was also a painter, began writing under the name "Palette" for the *Vancouver Daily Province.* A dapper individual who sported a cane, cape and jauntily angled hat, he had a style of writing that was both insightful and flamboyant.

A firm believer that art was "a vital and elevating force in the life of the individual and in the progress of the nation,"[12] Mildred encouraged Vancouverites to visit their art gallery. She reassured, "It is not a secret or mysterious place and you need go through no dark, devious byways to find it." She further explained that visitors would find "things that may seem queer, even distorted, but who... has ever yet attained to the full perfection of the vision which appeared before their eyes?"[13] Mildred's reviews ranged from children's school exhibitions to that of local amateur art clubs to more professional work shown at the VAG. Most of her comments were positive and heartening: "She liked to contextualize an artist's work, giving background or historical information, as well as discussing the art. She also tried to support everyone's efforts, sometimes going to great lengths to find a positive comment to make."[14] While Palette kept to safe ground, never commenting on the continuing squabbles amongst the arts community and staying clear of controversial remarks, Mildred never shied from such discussions.

Mildred also became a spokesperson for an atypical exposition, sponsored by the Labour Arts Guild in 1944 and 1945. Its president (1948–1953), John Goss, was a writer, musicologist and Marxist who "promoted socialist realism in the arts."[15] The aims of the organization were to encourage amateur and professional artists to identify with and "promote, develop and encourage the... arts as democratic forces in social, educational and cultural progress through association, participation and enjoyment of all people, irrespective of race, creed, class or color."[16] Those goals must have resonated for Mildred as they reiterated the objectives of her alma mater, Olivet College.

Those ideals also attracted the likes of poet Dorothy Livesay, architect Ross Lort, artist Una Bligh Newman and Claude Donald of the National Film Board. Although to all appearances a moderate individual with friends in both the B.C. Social Credit Party and the federal Conservative Party, Mildred always championed those she considered oppressed. Following the economic stresses of the Depression, and the pressures for high productivity during World War II, she, like many others, believed that working conditions and wages needed improvement. Mildred hoped that labour themes, as reflected in the work of amateur and professional artists, would encourage "politically and culturally progressive forces throughout the community."[17] She further stressed that an emphasis on work motifs would encourage artists to focus on subjects of human endeavour, which had long been neglected in favour of landscape themes in Canadian art.

Representing the Labour Arts Guild, Mildred successfully approached the VAG executive regarding a non-juried exhibition with work as the theme. Previously, in 1942, at Mildred's urging, the VAG had exhibited a collection of reproductions painted in the United Soviet Socialist Republic from 1917 to the 1940s.[18] In 1944, British Columbia at Work was held at the VAG (November 21 to December 10). A second exhibition was held in 1945, but the development of the Cold War and the perceived threat of communism brought about the dissolution of the Labour Arts Guild and artistic interest in social realism. Interestingly, the VAG's exhibition committee (Lawren Harris, Jock Macdonald and W.P. Weston) approved the Guild's exhibitions because they felt the presentations would "dispel the impression, of course entirely erroneous, that the Art Gallery exists to serve the interests of a privileged few."[19]

Erroneous or not, that impression long lingered in the city. John Vanderpant had complained of petty jealousies, conflicting factions and favouritism among the arts community during the 1930s, and nearly thirty years later (1962), painter Frank Molnar suggested that the Gallery was "lacking public support" and experiencing financial problems as a result of artistic "snobbery" in its selection practices.[20] In 1944, letters to the editor by many artists in the local newspapers indicated the dissatisfaction with and resentment toward the juries of the Annual B.C. Artists Exhibition at the VAG. In particular, numerous artists believed that representational art was being overlooked for more avant-garde work. They also charged that gallery members were selected over non-members. A number of "rebels," who felt their art had been discriminated against, set up an alternative exhibition at the small Dorbil Gallery on Granville Street.[21] Accusations and counter remarks ran in the papers from the end of September into the beginning of December.

That same year, Mildred (a member of the hanging committee) reviewed the unique venture that she had helped bring about: the one hundred and fifty works displayed in British Columbia at Work (VAG, 1944). She enthused, "This is one of the most significant exhibits ever held here being strongly reminiscent of Russia's Art for the People policy. It has the live, breezy, robust quality of things that are both democratic and popular." She felt strongly that the work of the common person could achieve a successful "creative effort." She further stressed that all submissions had been hung and "the amount of inferior material is surprisingly small, and the general standard is certainly higher than the majority of B.C. exhibitions." Mildred also took an unsubtle poke at artists whom she felt were motivated by new movements simply because they were popular:

> Artists who subscribe to the various "isms" can do absolutely anything and say that is what they saw, but here the element of truth cannot be flouted as these pictures are dealing with that most difficult and implacable problem—the human form and its activities.[22]

Like many artists of the day, Mildred was torn between her training and new trends. In 1947, her reaction to some experimental work was frank and unequivocal: "If artists expressed themselves verbally with the same degree of profanity that they use with a brush, jail space would be at a premium."[23] If her editor liked controversy, Mildred, in her role of critic, was providing the *Vancouver Sun* and the community with disputatious material. On the other hand, Mildred was not dismissive of all avant-garde art. From the 1940s through the 1950s, she positively reviewed work that fell into many of the "isms." In 1944, when commenting on the abstract work of S.E. Brunst, she wrote, "People who are interested in ultra-modern art will find many things here to intrigue them."[24] While Mildred was never overly fond of abstraction, particularly abstract expressionism, local proponents such as Jack Shadbolt, B.C. Binning and Gordon Smith usually garnered favourable reviews from her. In 1957, as Smith's work was reflecting increasing abstract influences, she wrote that his paintings were "inventive and exploratory, with rare command of contour and keenly perceived tonal balance." She concluded that his canvasses "all indicated intelligent objective analysis which emerges as the true creative activity of a gifted and sincere artist."[25]

Over the years, the arts community grew more and more divided between those who supported more traditional styles and those keen on more experimental influences. The latter had the support of the VAG, the Vancouver School of Art, the

University of British Columbia and artists such as B.C. Binning, Lawren Harris and Jack Shadbolt. Animosities continually simmered and boiled in a community divided. Poet Marya Fiamengo (wife of artist Jack Hardman) remembers "vividly" that those who favoured abstraction "were belligerent and outspoken, [and] there was resistance to that, especially by the public." Fiamengo further recalls that Mildred had her detractors and supporters, and artist Joe Plaskett was one who "defended Mildred." He maintained her work "had merit, while others were holding their noses and looking away. She was a highly admirable woman who was treated unfairly by the avant-garde establishment... [who] were jealous. The public liked her. She was a pioneer of a sort."[26]

Exacerbating the tensions in the arts community was the fact that there were few venues where artists could exhibit and sell their work; most sold from their home studios. There was little financial assistance, and there were limited patrons in the young city. The VAG's Women's Auxiliary started an annual exhibition titled Do You Own a Canadian Painting? (1949–1961) as a means of drawing people to the gallery and encouraging the sale of work by local artists. Prices were affordable, ranging from $10 to $1,000. Gordon Smith recalls that one year he and Bruno Bobak each sold a painting at that exhibition; with $35 each in their pockets, they splurged and bought themselves new tweed jackets.[27]

Throughout her career, Mildred was concerned about keeping public art galleries accessible to artists and the general public: she thought they should feel welcomed and engaged by such institutions. With that in mind, it seems, Mildred took it upon herself to voice the views of the disgruntled. Even though her painting Fort Steele in the Kootenay had been displayed, in a December 1950 column, she noted that only one hundred and fifty out of five hundred submissions for that year had been chosen for the 19th Annual B.C. Artists Exhibition at the VAG. She queried why works were being turned down under the explanation that there was not enough space, yet the jurors were hanging their own paintings and those of their spouses.[28] Furthermore, while in one column she praised two Jack Shadbolt watercolours (Autumn Grasses and Forms for Winter) as displaying "a wealth of imagination,"[29] in another she charged that "the work of serious-minded artists... should claim more attention than the subconscious phantasmagoria of immature minds."[30] The latter comments were mainly directed at two canvases by Jerry Brusberg, an abstract expressionist working in the style of Jackson Pollack.

Across the Inlet, n.d.
oil on board, 9¾" x 12¾"
PRIVATE COLLECTION

Lawren Harris, who headed the selection committee, defended the selections, explaining that "the best paintings in every style are chosen."[31] The director of the University of British Columbia Fine Arts Gallery, the editor of *The Ubyssey* (University of British Columbia student paper), several students and an English lecturer wrote they had "long regretted the bigoted, uninformed and misleading content" of Mildred's reviews.[32] In response to radio remarks the amateur painter Eileen Laurie made in support of Mildred's criticisms, painter Molly Lamb Bobak claimed, "Both showed a small-town, narrow point of view and a complete lack of understanding."[33]

Mildred stayed out of the brouhaha, but a caterwaul of letters carried on for the rest of the month. M. Denton-Burgess, another painter, was among the most vociferous. He offered congratulations to Mildred for not being "afraid to speak the truth" and to the *Vancouver Sun* for being "willing to publish it."[34] In another letter, he suggested that the VAG was being overly influenced by staff of the Vancouver School of Art, Lawren Harris did not "tolerate criticism" and paintings were being rejected because they were not modern enough.[35]

Abstraction was new and exciting to many local artists, but others dismissed or vehemently disliked the movement. Gordon Smith recalls that Mildred's comments added fuel to the local "divisions in the arts scene," and Mildred "was not alone" in her criticism or dislike of some abstract art. According to Smith, numerous artists, including Alister Bell, Orville Fisher, E.J. Hughes, Joe Plaskett and W.P. Weston, were among those who "didn't like it either. I remember slamming abstract art myself and saying it was all a joke." Smith changed his mind after a 1951 exhibition at the University of British Columbia, curated by Renee Bloue, that contained work by major abstract artists such as Willem De Kooning and Jackson Pollock: "It was then I realized how great the work was." That summer, Smith enrolled at the San Francisco Art Institute and then "became very abstract." He was encouraged by his friends and mentors, Jack Shadbolt and B.C. Binning. However, he remembers showing an abstract painting to another friend, W.P. Weston, who responded: "Well, Gordon, you can always turn the canvas over and paint again."[36]

During the 1950s, Mildred remained resistant to much of the highly abstract and experimental paintings produced locally. Interestingly, when an exhibition of German expressionism came to Vancouver in 1950, she praised the work for its "inner quality of rugged honesty and intellectual integrity" and described the paintings as "powerful, without being radical, pedantic or offensive."[37] "As well, she often responded favourably to the "lyrical, painterly abstraction with a landscape refer-ence"[38] that predominated in Vancouver. Semi-abstract references are also found in some of her paintings.

In February 1951, Mildred was again sharply critical of some works exhibited at the VAG. While praising Jack Shadbolt's entries, she condemned the VAG for filling every room with "ultra-modern art."[39] In December of that year, in response to the 20th Annual B.C. Artists Exhibition, Mildred charged that "a clique in the Vancouver Art Gallery is ministering to the vanity of a small minority of abstract artists. This is dictatorship of the most insidious kind." She further complained that jurors exhib-ited their own paintings, to which the director replied that it was a "courtesy" to allow the jurors to hang two works.[40] Again, a debate raged in numerous letters to the editor.

Jack Shadbolt then added his voice to the controversy. He viewed himself as Mildred's "nemesis," and years later admitted that he wrote "nasty letters"[41] to the local newspapers and would "attack" Mildred "on a regular basis."[42] In private, he also had a "rude nickname" for her.[43] Mildred was sixty years old in 1950, and Shadbolt, and many of Vancouver's other younger and more experimental artists, may have viewed her as antiquated, thereby becoming dismissive of her art and views. Shadbolt was particularly incensed over Mildred's criticisms of the VAG and the resulting uproar in the local media. In a lengthy letter to the *Vancouver Sun* in January 1952, he called Mildred "shrewd," "old," a puffball who "would easily be blown away on any but a popular newspaper level," and "a laughing stock." Shadbolt described her as one who "babbles with spurious eloquence" on a "sniping, rabble-rousing level" and coun-seled, "Dethrone yourself, Milly!"[44] Perhaps Mildred felt vindicated in 1960 when Alan Jarvis, director of the National Gallery from 1955 to 1959, stated that he was "astonished" that the VAG had such "a poor collection."[45]

In spite of the furor, the VAG continued to acquire and exhibit work deemed to be modern and experimental. That policy did not quell further complaints from those who felt ostracized. A less obvious outcome to the fracas was that Mildred's work was never again accepted to the Annual B.C. Artists Exhibition held at the VAG. According to Reg Ashwell, "Mildred went from being the darling of the Vancouver Art Gallery to being shunned."[46] To this day, the VAG has only one Thornton painting, a portrait of Chief Willie Seaweed.[47]

Problems with the arts community did not stop Mildred from continuing her position as art critic, which she held until 1959. She felt marginalized after 1951; her work was considered out of date by those favouring abstraction, and she was viewed as eccentric for her fascination with aboriginal people and cultures. Ever-determined, Mildred found alternative venues in which to showcase her work. She continued to display one or two pieces (usually aboriginal portraits or aboriginal scenes that were not for sale) at the non-juried Annual Exhibition: B.C. Society of Fine Arts held at the VAG. She also held exhibitions in department stores, which sometimes showcased artwork. In 1958, as part of the Province's centennial celebrations, Mildred exhibited at the Hudson's Bay Company in both Vancouver and Victoria; she also had the portrait, *Mrs. Mary Moon*

Mrs. Mary Moon
(Kwakwaka'wakw)
circa 1950, oil on board
22½" x 16"
PRIVATE COLLECTION
JOHN CAMERON PHOTOGRAPHY

(Kwakwaka'wakw) shown in 100 Years of BC Art at the VAG. As she aged, undertaking exhibitions became more difficult. As one example of the support she received, for the 1958 showing at the Hudson's Bay Company auditorium, Mildred's friends from her numerous affiliations, including the PEO (Philanthropic Educational Organization) Sisterhood, Native Daughters and the Coqualeetza Fellowship, came to her aid, each group helping on different days.[48] In addition, her colleagues at the *Vancouver Sun* paid for the framing of several paintings. They were only too happy to assist a colleague whom they "love[d]... for her warm human understanding."[49] She also had work shown at the Commonwealth Institute Gallery in London, England, in 1959. Finally, for three weeks, Mildred's paintings (about one hundred and fifty) were "the feature attraction" of a June 1962 exhibition at the Oakridge Shopping Centre Auditorium. First Nations carvings were displayed, and dances were performed by students from St. Paul's Indian School, Chief Dan George and members of the Squamish community.[50] At age seventy-two, Mildred was still making and showcasing B.C. history.

NINE

Stepping Outside the Norm

Mildred had an extraordinary talent for connecting with dynamic individuals, particularly women. She came to know and befriend Edith Clark, a Vancouver School of Art graduate and a long-time art dealer. Mildred's paintings became a regular fixture on the walls of Clark's Gallery of B.C. Arts, situated from 1961 to 1982 on the corner of Chilco Street and Georgia Street at the entrance to Stanley Park. With two thousand feet of floor space, the gallery was always "filled to overflowing with… something… to suit every artistic taste" and wallet.[1] Pottery, jewelry, paintings, sculptures (metal, stone and wood), weavings and First Nations masks and totems filled the premises from its grass-matting floors to the ceiling.

Leonard Woods, a retired Vancouver School of Art instructor (1945–1954) and art historian (1959–1969), never met Mildred but saw many of her watercolour landscapes on display in the Gallery of B.C. Arts:

> Mildred was a strong artist, forthright and very competent. I don't think she has ever been accorded the recognition that is her due. What is lacking is a record of

‹ *Entrance to Lions Gate Bridge,* n.d., watercolour
6⅝" x 8⅝"
PRIVATE COLLECTION
DAN FAIRCHILD PHOTOGRAPHY

Trees, n.d., watercolour
9⅝" x 13⅝"

PRIVATE COLLECTION

DAN FAIRCHILD PHOTOGRAPHY

her achievement. If that were done, we would recover an important painter and a record of a lot of Vancouver [and B.C.] that has disappeared.[2]

For nearly ten years, Woods gave weekly Monday afternoon art history lectures at Clark's gallery. He believes Clark had two "great achievements." She sold local pottery and "worked hard to get the British Columbia Potters' Guild underway. She featured big exhibitions of their work and got them on their feet." Woods views Clark's other achievement as becoming "great friends with the First Nations carvers, and she featured West Coast Indian art before anybody else did."[3] Writer Mona Fertig worked for Clark in 1968 and notes in her book on her father, artist George Fertig, that the carvers would "sometimes have a feast in her honour."[4]

Danny Kostyshin was employed by Clark for one summer (1970) and says she supported artists not only financially but "on an emotional level." He describes Clark as "a folksy Peggy Guggenheim" and as being "well-respected…. Edith was the only one who purchased work outright in those days [late 1960s]. She gave half cash, and the rest was on consignment. She was a godsend."[5]

Eric Schou Hammerum was first employed by Clark in 1972, working Saturdays and Sundays, "our big tourist days." They became close friends. When the building housing Clark's gallery was purchased by developer Stanley Ho in 1982, Schou Hammerum helped Clark operate the business from the basement of her West Vancouver home. He remembers that

> all the Native artists loved her. They would bring their families and sell their carvings to Mrs. Clark. She would serve tea. When she died, the Native community was very sad because she was one of the dealers who dealt with them respectfully and kindly.[6]

Schou Hammerum further recounts that Clark was fond of Mildred and the two women had "some very good talks." Through Clark, he "first learned [some]… artists… were deliberately shut out [of the Vancouver Art Gallery] or their efforts were thwarted."[7]

⌃ *Untitled,* n. d. water-colour, REPRODUCED FROM KODACHROME SLIDE IN THORNTON FAMILY COLLECTION, DIGITALLY RESTORED BY JANET DWYER

⌃⟨ *Untitled,* n. d. water-colour, REPRODUCED FROM KODACHROME SLIDE IN THORNTON FAMILY COLLECTION, DIGITALLY RESTORED BY JANET DWYER

Whispers have long abounded that Jack Shadbolt and his wife, Doris, intensely disliked Mildred and that their influence kept her work out of the VAG. Mildred's friend, Reg Ashwell, her son Jack and several others believe this to be the case. Professor and biographer David Stouck describes Doris Shadbolt's evaluation of Mildred's work. He attended a lecture on Emily Carr given by Doris at West Vancouver's Silk Purse Gallery sometime during the early 1990s[8] and recalls an exchange:

> After she finished her talk on Emily Carr, a man in the audience asked if Doris thought Mildred Valley Thornton wasn't as good as Carr in the way she portrayed Native people. Shadbolt simply said, "No." I wasn't quite satisfied with this answer, so I approached her afterwards with my observation that Thornton did something different from Carr; aside from the portraits, she painted the activities of the Natives; at work carving, preparing salmon, whaling, readying the potlatch—and I also mentioned the painting of the Plains women erecting tee-pees. Shadbolt's reply was simply, "Thornton had no vision; she was an illustrator at best." I let it go at that, though I did not agree with her.[9]

Nor do others agree with Doris Shadbolt. Mildred's paintings are proficient enough for exhibitions and sales in prominent private galleries and auctions across Canada, including Montreal's Galerie Walter Klinkhoff and Sotheby's Art Auction House. Her work is also housed in some of Canada's most prodigious art institutions and frequently appears in the Heffel Gallery auctions in Canada. In 1990, Anthony Westbridge held an exhibition of Mildred's work. Vancouver journalist Jill Pollack wrote that Mildred's paintings had "enormous historical value." Pollack also recognized that Mildred "was a woman who stepped outside the norm because she so profoundly believed it was her place to do so."[10]

At Westbridge's invitation, Ian Thom, senior curator, historical, at the Vancouver Art Gallery, also attended the 1990 retrospective. Westbridge recalls that Thom swept around the exhibition and was out the door. Westbridge shakes his head in frustration when he notes that other institutions have Thornton's work, but her hometown gallery (the VAG) does not consider her paintings worthwhile.

In 1992, Maria Tippett published *By a Lady: Celebrating Three Centuries of Art by Canadian Women*. In the book's introduction, Tippett states that this country's "women artists have been ignored, forgotten and marginalized." She goes on to claim that her book "seeks to set the record straight."[11] However, while Mildred was

Fireguard, Saskatchewan
circa 1920, oil on canvas
24" x 30"
PRIVATE COLLECTION
DAN FAIRCHILD PHOTOGRAPHY

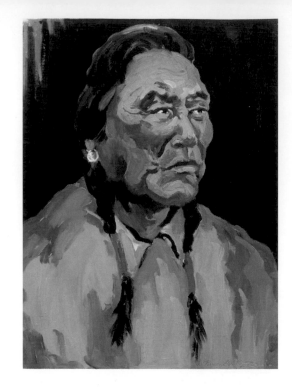

Captain Andrew Brown
(Haida), 1946, oil on
board, 24" x 18"
PRIVATE COLLECTION
DAN FAIRCHILD PHOTOGRAPHY

Tom Turn-Up-Nose
(Siksika), 1942 oil on
board, 24" x 18"
PRIVATE COLLECTION
DAN FAIRCHILD PHOTOGRAPHY

already listed in several provincial, national and international indexes of female art-ists, Tippett excluded any mention of Mildred.

In 1993, twenty-six years after Mildred's death, Brooks Joyner became the director of the Vancouver Art Gallery. He wanted to acquire some of Mildred's work:

> I thought she was an important early-mid 20th century Canadian painter with a special contribution to the recording of the Native peoples and landscape of Canada and particularly British Columbia.
>
> I discovered Mildred Valley Thornton's work as I studied Canadian art history as director of the art gallery at the University of Calgary and later adjunct profes-sor at the University of Alberta. I was immediately taken by her bold color, grasp of compositional elements and marriage of both semi-abstract and naturalistic qualities....
>
> Thornton's work resonated with me. It was crisp and robust, and it had strong content that was well understood by the painter. Her work was purposeful and at times "monumental" even though the canvases were not large. I remembered her work when I returned to Vancouver... and was even more intrigued by the fact that she was also a writer/art critic.[12]

In 1994, Anthony Westbridge invited Joyner to view Thornton's work. In a letter to Westbridge, Joyner described the paintings as "remarkable," but stated he was

> perplexed by the fact that she has received such little recognition and interest from the Vancouver Art Gallery, given her lengthy career, the subject of her art and the remarkable contribution that she made to the Vancouver arts scene. I will be speaking with the curators about... how she fits into the future of the Gallery's collection.[13]

Joyner also indicated his interest in a possible exhibition of Mildred's work. Seven months later (January 1995), he wanted "to work with [Westbridge] to establish a small, but comprehensive, Thornton collection in the VAG."[14] Joyner further indicated his interest in having the Gallery acquire five of Mildred's oil paintings: *Marine Building* (circa 1940s), *Kwakiutl Warrior Dance* (1945), *Bralorne Mine* (circa 1949), *Temples of Commerce* and *The Grocer's Shop* (Richmond).

The curators did not agree with Joyner. He explains:

> Given the narrow collecting habits of the VAG at the time of my tenure there, I was largely handcuffed in that effort by what can politely be called myopia. I view Thornton as a very remarkable Canadian artist and cultural figure whose passion for her subject and for the furtherance of the study of art was truly important and genuine. That she was rejected by the province of British Columbia and embittered at the time of her death is a sad legacy that needs to be corrected."[15]

Westbridge subsequently met a couple who "loved Mildred's work." They wanted to purchase *Temples of Commerce* to donate to the VAG. Westbridge says the potential benefactors' only proviso was that the institution had to agree to exhibit the work. The VAG would not commit to the condition, and the donation fell through.

Westbridge later had discussions with the National Portrait Gallery. Senior Curator Eva Major-Marothy, who describes Mildred's work as "accomplished,"[16] wrote Westbridge in 2004. She stated that the acquisition committee, which Westbridge says included First Nations and other outside members, was interested in acquiring, by donation, eighty-seven portraits. After studying three samples, *Captain Andrew Brown* (1946), *Mrs. Captain Brown* (1946) and *Tom Turn-Up-Nose* (1942), Major-Marothy noted that the Portrait Gallery viewed the paintings as historically significant. Unfortunately, the acquisition never materialized.

Trees (Stanley Park)
1943, oil on board
11" x 14"
PRIVATE COLLECTION
PHOTO BY JANET DWYER

Westbridge explains:

It was made clear from the beginning that the National Portrait Gallery did not
have the funds to purchase the portraits. Instead, they suggested that I might
look for a benefactor to acquire and donate the work. At the time there were
two prominent collectors of Mildred's work who were seriously considering the
donation idea. However, the less-than-advantageous tax laws of the day as they
pertained to donations, coupled with the National Portrait Gallery's loss of its
projected new home in the old American Embassy in Ottawa, ultimately meant
that it all went nowhere.

Westbridge says he has an English client who insists that, if Mildred were British,
her stature would be such that most private collectors would not be able to afford her
work. Another British collector has been acquiring Thornton paintings from various
sellers for years. She has twenty-five, which include portraits and landscapes, watercolours and oils.

An American collector says initially she "really didn't know anything about
Mildred" or early Canadian female artists.

It was through Ian Sigvaldason [Pegasus Gallery of Canadian Art] that I learned that these women have never received the recognition they deserve; only Emily Carr is known internationally. I thought the work of those early artists would be a good investment. Rather than putting money into stocks, I decided to invest in something I could enjoy; plus, I love the paintings that I have.[17]

In 1999, Mildred was made an Honorary Member of the Canadian Portrait Academy. That association classifies her as one of Canada's Top 100 Portrait Artists of the twentieth century. The Academy's founder, Christian Cardell Corbet (PPCPA, CGAM, BAMS, FIDEM, FA, FRSA), first encountered Mildred's work in 1994. He was "immediately intrigued by her use of colour" and saw that

she was using the Royal Academy colour scheme taught during her training [cobalt blue, ultramarine, emerald green, madder or alizarin crimson, purple and earth colours such as ochres, umbers and siennas], which was well-received in its day, but is not used much anymore. I clearly saw an American colour influence in her palette as well. However, she adjusted her palette and would sometimes use black, which was something the Royal Academicians never did. The use of the colour black was frowned upon in art schools of the day because, quite simply, it can be achieved using dark blues and viridian greens. It was often taught that there was no such thing as true black or white, just variant tints and tones of other existing natural colours. I think her use of black was very bold. [John William Beatty, Mildred's instructor at the Ontario College of Art, was known to throw away students' tubes of black or white paint.] I think she used a #8 brush on most of her canvases, sometimes a #10. I don't think she used anything more than three brushes. That takes confidence.

Compositionally, Mildred knew how to paint a landscape. I think the style is of her era, and there are some influences from the Group of Seven and their contemporaries. It was wise for Mildred to paint landscapes because they guaranteed sales and acceptance.[18]

Although Mildred allowed her subjects to seat themselves, Corbet finds the poses to be

very traditional: most of them being seated, many posing to the left or right, the size of the canvas (mostly 20 x 16 or 24 x 20 inches) and mostly head and shoul-

Mildred Valley Thornton

ders. Her work was not original in its composition. I am not being rude: I am saying that the compositions of her portraits were part of her training. Mildred learned to document the countenance, the composition, the psychological state of the subject in a time frame of forty-five to sixty minutes. Through the years, she became more fluid with her brushstrokes, more confident. She was more adept at landscapes, but her most honest work is her portraits. I don't think there can be anything better in an artist's work than honesty. Mildred worked on emotion. You can see it. She captures something in her sitter's eyes that very few portrait artists of her time did. She captured not just the humility but also the pride of the First Nations peoples. That's what draws me to her work. She could create a psychological effect, in two or three brushstrokes, that other people working on the West Coast at her time were unable to do. If you're successful as a portrait artist, there's going to be a magic conveyed within that portrait: the portrait lives beyond the person's life and beyond the canvas.

Trees with Stump
n.d., oil on canvas
29" x 23½"
THORNTON FAMILY
PRIVATE COLLECTION
PHOTO BY JANET DWYER

Mildred was independent in her thinking, and she painted how she wanted to paint. She didn't let anybody stop her, which shows a strength I have seen so many times in our great Canadian women artists. I don't like the fact that she did not gain the recognition she deserved during her lifetime. I believe her work will gain greater recognition over time. I think it holds a place in Canadian art history already. Her work is a documentation of an era. I find it odd that Canadian art institutions aren't picking up more of Mildred's work. I think she should have received the Order of Canada, but she didn't live long enough.[19]

Achim (Cree), 1950
oil on panel, 20" x 16"
KEITH AND JUDY SCOTT
PRIVATE COLLECTION
DAN FAIRCHILD PHOTOGRAPHY

Mildred did receive international recognition in her lifetime, being made a Fellow of the Royal Society of Arts in 1958. While pleased with that honour, what she most desired, the preservation of her "Collection," eluded her.

TEN

Passionate and Incomparable

During the early 1950s, Mildred's personal life was enriched with the birth of two grandsons, John and Ralph. A granddaughter, Janet, was born in 1961. While John did not find her "an affectionately demonstrative" type of grandmother, he remembers her as warm and loving. John says he was also the "apple of her eye. She always made me an oatmeal bran loaf. I loved it."[1] In fact, Phyllis Thornton (Jack's wife), says both grandparents doted on her children.[2] According to John, his grandfather

was a very nice man, very Victorian, but he must have been flexible of mind to have permitted his wife to go off visiting the Natives for lengthy periods. She was an eccentric woman in what she did and liked, but not wildly so. I remember she had a full-size Native carving on the front verandah—a humanoid figure she called Obediah. She had all manner of Native artifacts in the house. I remember she had a headdress from the Plains Indians and one from the West Coast Salish, the type with a bird with a beak that moves. I thought it was pretty neat. She also

‹ Mildred and grandsons forming a human totem pole, 1959
IB MEYER-OBEL PHOTOGRAPHER

B.C. Coastal Scene,
Mountains and Sea
circa 1948, oil on canvas
30" x 38"
PRIVATE COLLECTION
DAN FAIRCHILD PHOTOGRAPHY

had a deerskin dress with fringes around it. There were puffin beaks on every fringe, and they would make clackety sounds when she wore it. She also told stories very well and was quite intense that way. Her stories fascinated me.

She was also very proper and quite prissy in her own way. I remember one day, when I was twelve or thirteen, we were talking about smoking. Offhandedly, I said I'd never smoke. On the spot, she pulled out her cheque book and wrote me a cheque for twenty dollars. That was quite a sum in those days, and I was surprised. It's a promise I have honoured to this day, so she'd be pleased with the outcome of that transaction. However, my current penchant for dark ale would be something she'd frown on.

For about a year and a half, when I was nine to ten years old, I would go to her old house and paint under her watchful eye. I still have a couple of the oil paintings. They are obviously kid's paintings, but they are pretty good. We also used to go for walks in Stanley Park. She liked to walk there, and we'd get nuts and feed the squirrels. I also remember going to the Squamish Indian Reserve with her one time.[3]

John Thornton, Mildred's husband, passed away in 1958. After bailing water out of the basement, the result of a flood, he took to his bed with pneumonia and died suddenly. Mildred was devastated: years later, she would write that she still missed her "pal."[4] In 1966, in the dedication to *Indian Lives and Legends*, she wrote his "PATIENCE, ENCOURAGEMENT AND CO-OPERATION MADE THE WHOLE PROJECT POSSIBLE."

Aware of her grieving, her son Maitland invited Mildred to England where he was residing. Mildred stayed until 1961. Unfortunately, unbeknownst to Mildred, her young grandson Ralph developed a terminal illness while she was in Britain. He died in 1960. In her sadness, Mildred painted a portrait from memory of little "Ralphy." She gave that painting to his parents.

After returning from England, Mildred wanted to have some special time with her grandson, John. He relates that, in 1962, she took him on a one-week cruise to Alaska "on a combination passenger/freighter called the *Northland Princess*. We stopped in places like Bella Coola and Ketchikan. It was a fun trip but an unusual thing to do in those days."[5] For probably the first time in several decades, Mildred traveled lightly, leaving her paint box and brushes behind.

While in Britain, Mildred had been plagued by failing health but buoyed by the attention she received. She had two solo exhibitions, both well reviewed, at the Commonwealth Institute Art Gallery in London (1959 and 1961). Having been inducted as a Fellow of the Royal Society of Arts in 1954, she presented a paper to the members titled "Indians of British Columbia" (1959) that was printed in the *Journal of the Royal Society of Arts* in February 1960.[6] Mildred was nominated and accepted into the august organization because of her support for First Nations. While she praised individuals, their history and customs, and was sincere in her affection for aboriginal people, Mildred did speak from a colonial perspective common to the time, stressing that First Nations needed "wise guidance, sympathy and genuine friendship in a partnership which has nothing but good to offer to all concerned."[7] She reiterated her belief that "the only effective and permanent way to better the lot of our native people is through education." She emphasized that "Indians require exactly the same things that we do: health, education, and an equal chance to make a living."[8]

As early as 1946, Mildred began seeking advice on selling her First Nations portraits as an artistic and historic collection. While she had offers from buyers in Great Britain, Germany and the United States, she did not sell any aboriginal portraits

because she wanted the work to remain in Canada and she did not want to break up the collection. Besides, in keeping with her belief that education would improve the well-being of Canada's First Nations, Mildred wanted a portion of any profit to be used for an aboriginal education fund.

In 1949, Mildred had six large paintings of aboriginal life and customs reproduced as cards by the Austin Marshall Company of Toronto and packaged in a box titled Children of the Sun. Her purpose is not clear: she may have wanted to generate some income to pay for the storage of her paintings, she may have wished to create more interest in her work, she may have wanted to showcase the traditional customs and ceremonies of aboriginal peoples of Western Canada or, a combination of the above. In a letter to Dr. W.E. Ireland, B.C.'s provincial librarian and archivist, she mentions that they are "gift cards which ought to have an appeal as tourist mementos."[9] Some of those boxes made their way into B.C. school libraries and teacher resource rooms. In 1980, there was a set in a rural school in the Cariboo-Chilcotin School District.[10] How long the boxed set was used, or in which capacity, is not known.

Throughout the 1950s, Mildred actively tried to place her collection in a B.C. gallery or museum. A 1956 memorandum from Dr. Harry Hawthorn, UBC anthropology professor, to the university's president, Norman MacKenzie, is disturbing. Hawthorn not only "strongly" advised against any purchase, but also stated they had "value in that they are fairly realistic portraits, but they lose some of this in being all somewhat stereotyped; everyone looks like everyone else's cousin at least, and with 273, that makes quite a formidable lot of repetition." He went on to say the university "could gain something by the purchase... of half a dozen." In conclusion, and in spite of his earlier dismissive comments, Hawthorn stated he would be interested in the whole collection if it were donated to the university.[11]

In 1958, one of Mildred's supporters, poet and VPS member Alwyne Buckley, wrote MacKenzie, recommending that the university should take the opportunity "to acquire a permanent, unique and very representative memorial of our early history." Buckley goes on to say that "the individuals LIVE on the canvas" and that the work "could never be duplicated."[12] Shortly after, Hawthorn sent MacKenzie another memorandum. This time he stated, "The portraits have undoubted value as part of the provinces [sic] historical record. They have a strong, though rigid, quality. Unfortunately, they are not very accurate representations, nor do I regard them as major artistic achievements." He noted that they could be exhibited "in limited num-

‹ *Mrs. Andy Frank*
(Kwakwaka'wakw), 1952
oil on board, 22½" x 16"
PRIVATE COLLECTION
DAN FAIRCHILD PHOTOGRAPHY

▲ *Pretty Kangaroo Woman*
(Kainai), 1941
oil on board, 24" x 18"
PRIVATE COLLECTION
DAN FAIRCHILD PHOTOGRAPHY

▲▸ *Chief Herbert Johnson*
(Kwakwaka'wakw), 1946
oil on board, 30" x 22"
PRIVATE COLLECTION
JOHN CAMERON PHOTOGRAPHY

bers with other historical portraits and with similar materials in occasional exhibitions, or with the [George] Clutesi and [Judith] Morgan paintings… but perhaps they would belong more properly in the Art Gallery." However, Hawthorn again states that if a donor, in this case Buckley, wished to make a gift, then UBC would take the work. He suggested the low sum of $2,000, as "token monetary recognition" for the collection.[13]

On August 8, 1958, Ian McNairn, chairman of UBC's Warden's Committee on University Art, wrote MacKenzie regarding a Thornton acquisition. While on the one hand he states that her work was a "very worthwhile endeavour which should not be belittled or overlooked," the rest of his comments sound similar to those of Doris Shadbolt:

> There is a limited, pedantic ability in her drawing but her sense of colour and sensitivity to nature, to my mind, have never advanced beyond the most sentimental level. I have not seen one of her paintings… which I would accept as a competent painting or as an adequate illustration.
>
> I regret having to say this so bluntly but I feel that the acquisition of a collection of this sort, whether through purchase or by gift, might be most embarrassing for the University. I feel that in a case of this kind certain standards must be

established…. If we are going to try to encourage an understanding and appreciation of good painting, we must always be cautious of the examples which we have available for public view and for student reception.[14]

Ironically, the University of Victoria found Mildred's work to be so exemplary that in 1985 they named a President's Scholarship in her honour.[15]

The final discussion between MacKenzie and Hawthorn seems to have occurred on May 29, 1961. Hawthorn again wrote MacKenzie, this time noting his admiration for "the strength of Mrs. Thornton's intention" and her "considerable" achievement; he adds insightfully that the portraits "will have value for younger Indians, especially in years to come." Rather than a purchase, however, he suggests that, should the Provincial Archives buy the paintings, "the [Anthropology] Museum might ask for the loan of a few… for display."[16]

Mildred was in her seventies, her health was failing, her finances were low, and she had to move from her large house to an apartment in the Kerrisdale area of Vancouver (where Jack and his family were living). She wrote numerous letters, desperately trying to find someone to keep her life's work intact. Friends and supporters also came to her aid. In a 1963 letter to the Hon. Wesley Black, B.C.'s provincial secretary, Mildred noted that, at its annual convention, the Provincial Council of Women had passed a resolution to "put before the [B.C.] government" a request to have her "unique collection" purchased for the province's "fine new museum."[17] Over a year later, September 5, 1964, Mildred again wrote the Hon. Wesley Black, stressing that her house was for sale, she was "just recovering from a long and severe illness," and she was undertaking "some drastic changes in… [her] life."[18] In August and September of that year, Mildred also wrote L.J. Wallace, the deputy provincial secretary. In her first letter, she enclosed a copy of the 1960 *Journal of the Royal Society of Arts*, which contained her acceptance lecture to that "august body."[19] The government officials seem to have used the excuse of being too busy to coordinate a meeting. Mildred diplomatically replied, "Indeed I do understand that it is difficult to get four busy people together for the purpose of coming to see my slides." Mildred then tried to further interest the government officials by offering the frames made for her 1958 Hudson's Bay centennial exhibition as well as her

Indian art—several very large carvings, a great many small ones, argillite poles, Haida engraved silver jewelry, about fifty baskets, a dress of smoked buckskin

trimmed with fringe and tiny deer hooves that belonged to Pauline Johnson…
my own beautiful white doeskin dress… [and] the finest button blanket.

She described the frames and artifacts as a "bonus because I would like to have all my things stay together."[20] In another letter to Wallace, Mildred asked to set up an appointment in Victoria and tried to press the government by stating that "the National Museum is definitely interested—also cultural groups in Saskatchewan and Alberta who will be sending representatives to see me later in the month."[21]

Not having any luck with B.C. government officials, Mildred sought the assistance of her friend, Marius Barbeau. She told him:

> It is comforting to know of your interest in the work to which I have devoted the
> best years of my life…. As you say it should be preserved intact as a national heri-
> tage, a record of a colorful era in Canadian life."[22]

In a follow-up letter to Barbeau, Mildred stated that she would like to show him her whole collection as

> we have the same affection and understanding of our Native people. I am proud
> indeed to count so many of them as my friends…. I deeply appreciate your inter-
> est in my work and am hopeful that it may be preserved for the nation. So many
> appeals have gone out for various groups and individuals who should be inter-
> ested in such an enterprise, but nothing concrete… so far, yet it could happen
> any time.[23]

Her optimism and drive to find the portraits a home were never-ending. While the government remained cool, Mildred employed her incredible networking skills.

In 1965, Reg Ashwell wrote a lengthy letter to Wallace asking if the government would consider purchasing Mildred's work, including her scenes of First Nations life, as a centennial project. He suggested that the provincial government had not

> truly grasped the importance of this collection. The age-old ceremonies and
> dances of our native Canadian Indians come to thrilling life on the artist's can-
> vas in bold exciting color. The collection, properly housed in a gallery, would be a
> tremendous public attraction and a real asset to British Columbia.

Ashwell went on to propose that the images would be valuable for reproduction on travel brochures or school textbooks. He further indicated that the First Nations villages Mildred had painted had mostly disappeared and most of the totem poles had fallen over "and many of the old chiefs and historically colorful Indians she painted have passed away." He ended by stressing that Mildred's "greatest wish" was for B.C. to have the collection. Reg suggested that a reasonable offer be made "as Mrs. Thornton has an overwhelming urge to help the Indians with whatever money she can." Reg reminded Wallace that the paintings are "a precious heritage we cannot afford to do without…. These paintings are not only fascinating works of art—they are history! So let's get them while we have the chance!"[24]

Even though Ashwell warned that a German museum was trying to purchase *The Hao Hao Dance of the Bella Coolas,* the government indicated no interest in the paintings for a centennial project and suggested that the Provincial Museum should be contacted. Wilson Duff, the Curator of the Anthropology Museum wrote Dr. G.C. Carl, the Director of the Provincial Museum's Department of Recreation and Conservation, that the paintings

> are not the accurate historical records which they are claimed to be. They are artistic compositions rather than true illustrations, and (especially the scenes reconstructed only from Indian informants' descriptions) they contain many details which are probably incorrect. In most instances we have old photographs which are superior as records.[25]

There are troubling aspects to Duff's remarks. He is not only questioning Mildred's accuracy but "the Indian informants' descriptions." As well, he is not even sure that the accuracy is to be disputed saying they are "probably incorrect." Indeed, Mildred's description of a Kwakwaka'wakw initiation ceremony (*Warrior Dance*) contains the elements described by the 1876 eye-witness account of the coming of age of Johnny Chickite by Dr. W. Wymond Walkem.[26] Furthermore, as has been pointed out in other studies, artistic licence was taken by many artists who visited aboriginal sites, including Emily Carr, and that has not prevented their acquisition.

Duff did concede that the portraits were valuable because most of the people had died and Mildred had recorded information about them. He describes the portraits as "mostly attractive character studies; however… judging from the individuals known personally to me, the likenesses are not very exact."[27] Duff seems to have preferred the *truth* of photography, but as history has shown, even that medium was often manipulated, exaggerated, distorted or incorrect.

Dr. Ireland, the provincial librarian and archivist, visited Mildred in September 1965 to consider a purchase of her book collection, Indian artifacts and paintings. He wrote Mildred that the government would likely be interested in some of the artifacts; as he already had the same books, he suggested that local book dealers would "be delighted to have them." Regarding the paintings, he was only interested in those pertinent to B.C., but he "would like to have some… not only because of subject matter but also as examples of your work as an artist."[28] After the visit, Mildred wrote Ireland that she was

> dismayed at the suggestion that I part with a *few* of them. However, I am willing to reconsider this matter in the hope that the government will eventually purchase the entire B.C. collection for our own province where they will be of great interest to future generations.

Mildred said, if Ireland informed her of his selection, she would "quote a fair price and get them out of the vaults."[29] She was asking $200,000 for the entire collection. The resulting offer is unknown, but Jack recalls that it was quite low. Mildred reacted sharply, and in October sent Ireland a note of apology for her "abrupt reply…. I was aghast at the thought of breaking up the collection after keeping it together at the cost of so much effort and sacrifice." However, after considering the matter, she did indicate that they might still "be able to work out an agreeable arrangement."[30]

Mildred did sell many artifacts to the Provincial Museum and told Ireland, "It really grieved me to part with so many treasures that have been part of my life for so long. I loved them all, and the people who made them, but it is satisfying to know they are where they will be preserved and appreciated."[31] Jack Thornton says Mildred was unwell and under "emotional strain" when she sold her artifacts. After recovering somewhat, she much regretted the low price she received but was more distraught at losing the many mementos she so cherished.

Mildred continued to enlist any help she could find. In June 1965, M.Y. Williams, UBC professor emeritus, wrote the Hon. Wesley Black, suggesting that Mildred's approximately two hundred B.C. portraits might be purchased as "an historic and educational unit." He also suggested that the Alberta government might purchase the more than sixty portraits of its peoples and Saskatchewan might like the thirty-five or so of its First Nations ancestors. He stressed that, in spite of offers from museums in the United States and Germany, Mildred wanted to keep "this unique art

and anthropological collection" in Canada. Williams further suggested that financial assistance might be available from the Canada Council and the "new National Museum."[32]

By 1965, Mildred's optimism was waning. Her rigid desire to keep the collection intact was beginning to weaken. She wrote, "I suppose if it were desirable either of these collections [the prairie paintings and the B.C. paintings] could be sold separately." She further observed,

> I am an artist, not a business woman and often feel much in need of competent advice concerning these affairs. I would be glad to know of any dealers who would be interested in my special field, in case as a last resort I break up the collection.[33]

On July 30, 1965, Mildred wrote that Mr. Arima from the National Gallery had visited her, but no commitments to purchase the collection were made. Mildred lamented: "There have been many petitions from cultural groups and leading citizens here both to Ottawa and the B.C. Government to have them save this collection

Untitled, n d.
watercolour
7⅝" x 9⅝"
PRIVATE COLLECTION
DAN FAIRCHILD PHOTOGRAPHY

for posterity, but Canadians seem to be painfully unaware of our national heritage." She further noted that while "I never did the work with the object of making money" and for twenty-five years had paid to keep the work in a vault, she now needed "money and must make some arrangements concerning… [the paintings]."[34]

Mildred's situation became more and more desperate as her finances dissipated and her suffering from the physical fatigue and the excruciating bone and joint pain associated with her disease increased. Frantically "beset by many anxieties,"[35] she began a letter-writing campaign to such institutions as the Royal Ontario Museum, the Mendel Art Gallery and even a small Saskatchewan museum, the Pion-era, hoping they might be interested in purchasing the Saskatchewan art. Mildred hoped to sell the Saskatchewan portraits for $20,000, the Alberta for $40,000 and the B.C. for approximately $140,000.[36]

One of her strongest supporters was New Democratic MP Barry Mather. How he became involved is not known; they likely met because Mather was a journalist for the *Vancouver News Herald* during the 1940s and later for the *Vancouver Sun*. In a 1967 letter, Mildred mentions "the lovely visits we had in your lovely home." They also shared a dislike of cigarettes: Mather being one of the first MPS to suggest restrictions on cigarette sales, and he later advocated for a ban on cigarette advertising. In that same letter to Mather, Mildred complained that while many people think the collection should be kept in the country, "no one does anything about it. They all know about it in Victoria… but words are cheap." She lamented that, while Judy LaMarsh had once considered paying six million for a small Leonardo da Vinci painting, Canada's Heritage Minister "wouldn't pay a fraction of that amount for 300 paintings by a Canadian.[37]" Mildred also noted that Marius Barbeau had failed to interest the National Museum of Canada. From May until December 1967, Mather tried to find an institution to house Mildred's collection. A response from former UBC president Norman MacKenzie, then a Canadian senator, indicated that while he had been interested for more than fifteen years, his enquiries to well-known artists indicated that they did not consider the work as accomplished and they thought the asking price of $200,000 was too high. (The names of those well-known artists are unknown.) MacKenzie was willing, however, to get together with Mather to try to consider alternative acquisition solutions.[38] The two agreed the collection was culturally and historically significant. They did not consider $200,000 as unrealistic value, and they agreed that they might be able to solicit interest from a government agency or philanthropist.[39] Mildred was now extremely ill. On the very day of her death, Mather tried to interest L.J. Wallace. B.C.'s Deputy Provincial Secretary in using the newly announced Provincial Fund for Culture to purchase the collection because "there is nothing else like this in North America."[40] However, it seems that the only serious institutional consideration ever given to the acquisition of the Collection was through donation or "token monetary recognition."[41]

In her last days, Mildred's physical suffering was matched by her emotional anguish. She was tormented by the realization that her Collection was not going to remain intact in a Canadian institution and that she would not be able to leave a monetary donation for a First Nations educational fund. According to Jack, Mildred's pain was becoming so severe she could often only scream. Understandably distressed, on June 12, 1967, she added a codicil to her will that her paintings should be sold in one large auction or taken to the dump, have gasoline poured over them and be set aflame. She lamented: "If 35 years of devotion to my country means nothing while I am alive, it is better that no record of it remain after I am gone."[42] Mildred died on July 27, 1967, and after her funeral at St. Paul's Anglican Church, Jack and Maitland were relieved to discover that the codicil had not been properly witnessed. Jack says he never could have fulfilled his mother's final, distraught request.

For the next four months, Mather continued in his efforts to place the paintings in an institution. He again approached the provincial librarian, who again declined on the grounds that "we have had several experts advise us as to their anthropological significance and artistic merit, and the reports have never been such as to encourage our acquisition."[43] Mather countered, "Opinions may differ as to the cultural or historical value of the work... but it is, without question, unique and irreplaceable."[44] In the meantime, Senator MacKenzie approached three philanthropists to no avail, H.R. MacMillan and Walter Koerner in B.C. and Eric Harvey in Calgary.[45] Finally Arthur Laing, the Minister of Indian Affairs and Northern Development, was approached. While he was interested in acquiring "at least a part of this collection for the Indians of western Canada,"[46] again no money was available. A donation from Mildred's heirs was suggested. Finally, on December 18, 1967, Senator MacKenzie told Mather that the best advice for Mildred's sons was to sell the paintings for whatever price they could acquire.[47] At that point, Jack and Maitland were as discouraged as Mildred had been. They eventually began selling their mother's works through commercial galleries and auction houses.

Potlatch, Alert Bay
(Kwakwaka'wakw)
circa 1940, oil on
Masonite, 30" x 40"
ORIGINAL IN GLENBOW
MUSEUM, REPRODUCED
FROM KODACHROME SLIDE IN
THORNTON FAMILY PRIVATE
COLLECTION, DIGITALLY
RESTORED BY JANET DWYER

In justification of Mildred's own appraisal of the value of her work, just four years after her death, Torben Kristiansen of the Art Emporium wrote Jack that in his "considered opinion" a total of "330 large and 300 smaller" of Mildred's paintings had "a present replacement value of $269,800.00."[48] Based on recent sales figures and professional assessments, Westbridge estimates that Kristiansen's figure would be at least ten times that amount today. Why then, except for inclusion in a variety of artist dictionaries and indexes,[49] has Mildred been mostly ignored in historical accounts; why does no major public gallery or institution, other than the Glenbow Museum in Calgary, have a substantial collection of her work? Is it because Mildred's strongly worded criticisms of some abstract art and perceived Vancouver Art Gallery practices published in the *Vancouver Sun* incurred the wrath of some local artists? Or is it because representational art was no longer considered cosmopolitan enough when the tide of abstraction in the fifties and the experimental art of the sixties washed over the city? The obvious answer would be artistic and ideological differences but also appears to be a discomfiting mix of ambivalence, condescension and disregard. Thanks to the continuing insistence of learned voices, there is a growing clamor for Mildred's life-long, passionate and incomparable work to finally receive more recognition.

Today, the Glenbow Museum has a collection of seven paintings (the oils are *Haida Potlatch, Kwakiutl Winter Ceremonies, Potlatch in B.C., Chief's Council* and *Moraine Lake*; the watercolours are *View in the Rockies* and *Indian Village*). The McMichael Canadian Art Collection has a portrait of Mungo Martin and *Potlatch Houses, Stanley Park*. The National Gallery of Canada has *The Touchwood Hills*, the Vancouver Art Gallery has a portrait of Willie Seaweed and Simon Fraser University Art Gallery has three untitled landscapes (two watercolours and one oil on panel). B.C.'s Provincial Museum

Ceremonial Masks
(Kwakwaka'wakw), n.d.
oil on canvas, 29½" x 39½"
PRIVATE COLLECTION

has a portrait of Chief Dan Cranmer, and the B.C. Archives has a portrait of former MLA Tilly Jean Rolston and a boxed collection of First Nations scenes, Children of the Sun and C.D. Cowan's portrait hangs in Regina City Hall. The Canadian Pacific Railway has one oil, *Train, Canadian Pacific,* the Dresden Public Library has one portrait of Tom MacInnes, and The Fort, Museum of the North-West Mounted Police has one portrait of Sir Frederick Haultain. Except for a collection that Westbridge is still marketing, private collectors in Canada, Great Britain, the United States and possibly other countries now hold the majority of Thornton's work.

Since her death, Jack has tended his mother's estate, edited her manuscripts for publication, written introductions to her republished and posthumously published books and has done his best to keep art historians aware of her legacy. His brother Maitland passed away in 2010, still waiting for his mother's work to receive greater acknowledgement in Canada; Jack, Mildred's grandchildren, and her extended family are still waiting.

A poem written in her High School Composition Book, 1908 poignantly reflects Mildred's unrelenting spirit and all-consuming dedication to her work. Her teenaged insight now seems prescient.

What is my soul seeking?
That my heart cannot express
What is it that beckons and lures me
Illusions in myriad excess
Groping with teardimmed eyelids
I would grasp them for my own
But even fact surrenders to fancy
The bright winged vision is flown
So 'tis in the brightness of youthtide
So 'tis the mellow eve
We are madly to pursue but fleet phantoms
That a veil of mystery weave
Peace, sad soul, cease complaining
Take heart from thy efforts vain
For as sure as thou losest thy phantoms
So sure they will come again.

During her lifetime, Mildred was driven to create. Thanks in part to her fortitude and tenacity, and her husband's incredible support, she completed a distinctive body of work. Perhaps the passage of time and changes in social and cultural perspectives will now allow for a fresh appraisal of the work of this singular artist. Mildred's regional importance in B.C. and Saskatchewan, as well as her overall contributions to Canadian art, would then be more fully appreciated. Then, too, her significant literary and social contributions, including her place in Canadian women's history, would be valued.

Mildred's original and powerful paintings help us to understand, honour and commemorate the peoples and environments of our country. Her paintings (both portrait and landscape) transcend time and are a bridge between our past, present and the ever-changing aspects of Canadian culture. Her legacy is a distinctive and vivid expression of audacity, hope, integrity, joy and love. Hers were not "efforts vain." Mildred Valley Thornton's paintings stand as unique representations by a masterful artist.

Whytecliff, 1953
oil on board, 24" x 30"
THORNTON FAMILY
PRIVATE COLLECTION
PHOTO BY JANET DWYER

MILDRED VALLEY THORNTON

EXHIBITIONS

British Columbia Interior Scene, circa 1950
oil on board, 10" x 12"
PRIVATE COLLECTION
DAN FAIRCHILD PHOTOGRAPHY

1930 Solo exhibition, Hotel Saskatchewan, Regina
Canadian National Exhibition, Toronto

1931 Canadian National Exhibition, Toronto

1932 Canadian National Exhibition, Toronto
Royal Canadian Academy of Arts, Toronto

1933 61st Annual Exhibition of the Ontario Society of Artists, Art Gallery
of Ontario, Toronto

1934 Royal Canadian Academy of Arts, Toronto

1935 Hudson's Bay Company
4th Annual B.C. Artists Exhibition, Vancouver Art Gallery

1936 Solo exhibition, Vancouver Art Gallery
5th Annual B.C. Artists Exhibition, Vancouver Art Gallery

1938 7th Annual B.C. Artists Exhibition, Vancouver Art Gallery

1940 Frederick & Nelson Auditorium, Seattle, Washington
9th Annual B.C. Artists Exhibition, Vancouver Art Gallery
Christmas Exhibition, Vancouver Art Gallery

1941 Royal Canadian Academy of Arts, Toronto Solo exhibition, Vancouver Art Gallery
10th Annual B.C. Artists Exhibition, Vancouver Art Gallery

1942 Solo exhibition, Provincial Museum, Parliament Buildings, Victoria

32nd Annual Exhibition: B.C. Society of Fine Arts, Vancouver Art Gallery

1943 Solo exhibition, Vancouver YMCA – Spitfire Fund, Vancouver

33rd Annual Exhibition: B.C. Society of Fine Arts, Vancouver Art Gallery

12th Annual B.C. Artists Exhibition, Vancouver Art Gallery

1944 34th Annual Exhibition: B.C. Society of Fine Arts, Vancouver Art Gallery

1945 35th Annual Exhibition: B.C. Society of Fine Arts, Vancouver Art Gallery

14th Annual B.C. Artists Exhibition, Vancouver Art Gallery

1946 36th Annual Exhibition: B.C. Society of Fine Arts, Vancouver Art Gallery

Jubilee Exhibition, Vancouver Art Gallery

1947 Solo exhibition, Eaton Fine Art Gallery, Toronto

16th Annual B.C. Artists Exhibition, Vancouver Art Gallery

1949 Solo exhibition, Vancouver Art Gallery

39th Annual Exhibition: B.C. Society of Fine Arts, Vancouver Art Gallery

1950 40th Annual Exhibition: B.C. Society of Artists, Vancouver Art Gallery

19th Annual B.C. Artists Exhibition, Vancouver Art Gallery

1951 41st Annual Exhibition: B.C. Society of Artists, Vancouver Art Gallery

1952 42nd Annual Exhibition: B.C. Society of Artists, Vancouver Art Gallery

1953 43rd Annual Exhibition: B.C. Society of Artists, Vancouver Art Gallery

1954 44th Annual Exhibition: B.C. Society of Artists, Vancouver Art Gallery

1955 45th Annual Exhibition: B.C. Society of Artists, Vancouver Art Gallery

1957 47th Annual Exhibition: B.C. Society of Artists, Vancouver Art Gallery

1958 Solo exhibition, Hudson's Bay Company Auditorium, Vancouver
Solo exhibition, Hudson's Bay Company, Douglas Room, Victoria
100 Years of B.C. Art, Vancouver Art Gallery
48th Annual Exhibition: B.C. Society of Artists, Vancouver Art Gallery

1959 Solo Exhibition, Commonwealth Institute Art Gallery, London, England
49th Annual Exhibition: B.C. Society of Artists, Vancouver Art Gallery

1961 Solo exhibition, Mildred Valley Thornton: The Canadian Indian and
Other Paintings, Commonwealth Institute Art Gallery, London, England

1962 Solo exhibition, Oakridge Auditorium, Vancouver

1965 Solo exhibition, T. Eaton Company, Vancouver

1970 Retrospective, Art Emporium, Vancouver

1971 Saskatchewan Art and Artists, MacKenzie Art Gallery, Regina

1974 Contemporaries of Emily Carr in British Columbia, Burnaby Art Gallery,
Burnaby, B.C.

1977 Retrospective, Art Emporium, Vancouver

1978 Early Canadian Watercolours, Uno Langmann Ltd., Vancouver

1979 Retrospective, Masters Gallery, Calgary

1980 Retrospective, Gallery of B.C. Arts, Vancouver
Keenlyside Gallery, Vancouver

1985 Retrospective, Westbridge Fine Art, Vancouver
Retrospective, Butler Galleries, Vancouver
British Columbia Women Artists 1885–1995, Art Gallery of Greater Victoria
Art Gallery of South Okanagan, Penticton, B.C.

1986 Retrospective, The Pagurian Gallery, Toronto

1988 Retrospective, Westbridge Fine Art, Vancouver

1989 Assiniboia Gallery, Saskatchewan, Saskatchewan

1990 Contemporary and Historical Art from the Collection, Vancouver Art Gallery

1992 Retrospective, Westbridge Fine Art, Vancouver

1993 Retrospective, Westbridge Fine Art, Vancouver

1994 Retrospective, Westbridge Fine Art, Vancouver

1995 Early British Columbian Woman Artists, Heffel Art Gallery, Vancouver
Retrospective, Westbridge Fine Art, Vancouver

1997 Women's Work: Art by Women in the Glenbow Collection, Glenbow Museum, Calgary

1998 Winchester Galleries, Victoria

1999 Kw'achmixwáylh: Showing of the Pictures: Mildred Valley Thornton
Collection of Squamish Nation Ancestors' Portraits, North Shore Museum &
Archives/Squamish Nation, North Vancouver

2000 Retrospective, Westbridge Fine Art, Vancouver

2008 Canadian Women Modernists: The Dialogue with Emily Carr, Vancouver Art Gallery

Mildred Valley Thornton
circa 1920s
THORNTON FAMILY
PRIVATE COLLECTION
PHOTOGRAPHER UNKNOWN

PUBLIC COLLECTIONS

Glenbow Museum

McMichael Canadian Art Collection

National Gallery of Canada

Royal BC Museum

Simon Fraser Art Gallery

Vancouver Art Gallery

PRIVATE COLLECTIONS

Canada, England, United States

ACKNOWLEDGEMENTS

I am grateful to Mildred's son, Jack Thornton, for giving me access to his mother's paintings, papers, photographs and memorabilia. His recollections and insights were invaluable, as was his cheerful patience and that of his wife Phyllis. Special thanks to Mildred's grandchildren, Janet and John Thornton, and to Mildred's extended family (especially Lance and Ann Evoy, and Lara T. Evoy) for their indispensable assistance.

A special thank you to the private gallery owners who shared their time and insights: Gunter Heinrich (Winchester Galleries), Jeanette and Uno Langmann (Uno Langmann Limited), and Ian Sigvaldason (Pegasus Gallery of Canadian Art). My deepest gratitude to Anthony Westbridge (Westbridge Fine Art), who tolerated numerous e-mails, phone calls and several lengthy conversations with generosity and good humour.

Warmest thanks to the numerous individuals who granted me interviews, assistance with queries and general help, and access to documentation and private art collections. I also extend my gratitude to those affiliated with institutions that kindly provided their assistance. They are as follows: anonymous private collectors, Reg Ashwell, Lynn Austin (Ontario College of Art and Design), Unity Bainbridge, Shanna Baker (*British Columbia Magazine*), Sandra Bell (Library and Archives Canada), Kate Bird (*Vancouver Sun* and *Province*), Martha Black (Royal BC Museum), Alison Bridger, James and Katheryn Broughton, Linda Burns, Janine Butler (McMichael Canadian Art Collection), Canadian Broadcasting Corporation, Vanessa Campbell (Squamish Nation), Jennifer Carpenter (Heiltsuk Education Centre), Bert and Hana Clark, Jo-Anne Colby (Canadian Pacific Railway Archives), Adriana Contreras (SFU Art Gallery), Lance Cooper (B.C. Archives), Christian Corbet, Holly Dankert (School of the Art Institute of Chicago), Dennis Duffy (B.C. Archives), Moira Ekdahl (Vancouver

School District), Marya Fiamengo, Sharon Fortney, Phoebe Fox-Bekerman (Archives of Royal Society of Arts), Ivor and Maureen Frederiksen, Bonnie French, Louis Gagliardi, Sherrill Grace, Peter Haase, Eric Schou Hammerum, David Hancock and Hancock House Publishers, Marja Hendrick (Olivet College Archives), Charles Hill (National Gallery of Canada), Quyen Hoang (Glenbow Museum), Deborah Jacobs (Squamish Nation), Peter Jacobs (Squamish Nation), Brooks Joyner (Allentown Art Museum), Cheryl Karchut (Silk Purse Gallery), Danny Kostyshin, Krisztina Laszlo (UBC Museum of Anthropology Archives), Barry Link (*The Vancouver Courier*), Margaret Locke, Bob and Patricia Logie, Erika Luebbe (Legislative Library of B.C.), Stephen Lunsford, Ann McCall (Royal Canadian Academy of the Arts), Robert McKay, Margaret MacLean, Eva Major-Marothy (Portrait Gallery of Canada), Frank Molnar, Magdelena Moore (North Vancouver Museum and Archives), Arlene Maris (Chatham-Kent Public Library), Ib Meyer-Obel, David Neel, Theresa Neel, Mary and Phil Nuytten, Jo Rappaport, *Regina Leader-Post,* Letia Richardson, Norma-Jean Rideout (The Fort, Museum of the North-West Mounted Police), Karen Rothschild (University of Victoria), Cora Ryan, Jayce Salloum, Matthew Sams (School of the Art Institute of Chicago) Judy and Keith Scott, Kirsten Skov, Cheryl Siegal (Vancouver Art Gallery Library), Gary Sim, Gordon Smith, Squamish Nation, staff of the B.C. Archives, staff of the UBC Archives, staff of the City of Vancouver Archives, staff of the Vancouver Public Library, Don Stewart and the staff of MacLeod's Books, Audrey Stinson, David Stouck, Kim Svendsen (Vancouver Art Gallery), Derek Swallow (Royal B.C. Museum and Archives), Gillian and William Taylor, Maitland and Peggie Thornton and family, Debra Usher (*Arabella*), Catharin Vanderpant, Erwin Wodarczak (UBC Archives), Kiriko Watanabe (West Vancouver Museum), Nicholas Westbridge, Shay Wilson, Jonathan Wise (Canadian Museum of Civilization), Frank Wade, Leonard Woods, Glenn Woodsworth and anyone I may have inadvertently overlooked.

I deeply appreciate the support of my publisher, Mona Fertig. Thank you to Katherine Gordon for her comments. The excellent photographic reproductions of Thornton's paintings are the work of John Cameron, Janet Dwyer, Dan Fairchild and Pippin Lee. Highly valued are Jan Westendorp's book and cover designs, Judith Brand's copyediting and Sheilagh Simpson's indexing.

Love to my family, especially Alyssa, Gary and Kirk, for their assistance, encouragement and patience.

ENDNOTES

Where the original names used for portraits of individuals or First Nations peoples have changed or been corrected, the current usage appears in the text.

Unless otherwise indicated (in an endnote or the text), where multiple quotations (or references) from the same source appear in a paragraph or a block quotation, the last quotation (or reference) from that source will contain the appropriate endnote.

Unless otherwise indicted in an endnote, references to Mildred's unpublished writings, the diaries of Reverend D.A. MacLean and the author's interviews with Jack Thornton and Anthony Westbridge will appear in the text.

INTRODUCTION

1 Reg Ashwell, "Mildred Valley Thornton," *Arts West*, 4, no. 3 (May–June 1979), p. 30
2 A.K. Prakash, *Independent Spirits: Early Canadian Women Artists*, Ontario: Firefly Books, 2008, pp. 26, 28
3 Mildred Valley Thornton, *Indian Lives and Legends*, Vancouver: Mitchell Press, 1966, p. XIV
4 Reg Ashwell, "Tribute to a lady who painted Indians," *Vancouver Sun Leisure Magazine*, April 8, 1971
5 This book was republished under the title *Potlatch People: Indian Lives and Legends of British Columbia* (Hancock House, 2003); a second book, *Buffalo People: Portraits of a Vanishing Nation*, was posthumously published in 2000 (Hancock House).
6 Mildred's son, Jack Thornton, maintains that Mildred's Collection was only comprised of First Nations portraits. There is documentation, however, to indicate that during the mid-1960s Mildred considered her scenes of aboriginal life as also being part of the Collection. See chapter 10 for further discussion.
7 Ashwell, "Tribute to a lady"
8 Thornton, *Indian Lives and Legends*, dedication page
9 Mildred Valley Thornton, rough draft of unpublished, undated poem, Thornton family collection. Where Thornton's writings are unpublished, the author has taken the liberty of correcting typing or spelling errors.
10 In "B.C. Women Artists 1920 to 1950," in the exhibition catalogue *British Columbia Women Artists 1885–1985* (Art Gallery of Greater Victoria, 1985), p. 15, Roberta Pazdro included just a one-paragraph outline of Mildred's career, the most information on Thornton in any exhibition catalogue to date.
11 Thornton, *Indian Lives and Legends*, p. XIV

CHAPTER ONE: TO WALK WORTHILY

1 J.M. Thornton, "Family Background, JMT" unpublished family history, January 2006, p. 3, Thornton family collection
2 Mildred Valley Thornton, unpublished draft of "Introduction," *Indian Lives and Legends*, p. 5
3 E-mails to author from Linda Burns and Lance Evoy, a great-niece and great-nephew of Mildred Valley Thornton, January 17 and 21, 2011. The location of this corner is the southeast quarter of Lot 11, Concession 7, Dawn-Euphoria Township.
4 Author's conversations with Christian Cardell Corbet, 2009
5 E-mail to author from Linda Burns, forwarded by Lance Evoy, January 17, 2011
6 J.M. Thornton, "Family Background," p. 3
7 Thornton, unpublished "Introduction,"pp. 4–5
8 J.M. Bumsted, *A History of the Canadian Peoples*, Toronto: Oxford University Press, 1998, p. 246
9 J.M. Thornton, "Mildred Valley Thornton, FRSA, CPA 1890–967," unpublished biography, 2006, p. 1, Thornton family collection
10 J.M. Thornton, "Family Background," p. 3
11 Thornton, unpublished "Introduction," p. 5
12 From information and photocopies of 1907/1908, 1908/1909 and 1909/1910 Olivet College catalogues supplied by Marja Hendrick, Olivet College Archives, April 13, 2010, and October 25, 2010
13 Thornton, unpublished "Introduction," p. 6
14 From a handwritten poem in Mildred's High

School Composition Book. Unless otherwise indicated, all further references to Thornton's unpublished poems, lecture notes and unpublished writings are from the Thornton family collection.

15 Bumsted, *History of the Canadian Peoples*, p. 204

16 "Olivet College Mission Statement," accessed June 23, 2010, http://www.olivetcollege.edu/about/strategic_priorities.php

17 Thornton, unpublished "Introduction," p. 6

18 The Ontario College of Art and Design does not have records for its early years; therefore, the dates of Mildred's enrolment are unknown.

19 "Mildred Valley Thornton of B.C. Visits an Artist Friend in City," *Woodstock Sentinel,* July 25, 1961

20 Dorothy M. Farr, *J.W. Beatty 1869–1941,* Kingston: Agnes Hetherington Art Centre, Queen's University, 1981, exhibition catalogue, p. 25

21 Ibid., pp. 55, 65, 27

22 Mildred did not always title her landscape paintings. Titles used in other publications, or those used by family or art specialists, are those used by the author.

23 Unless noted by the author, all further references to the author's communications with Jack Thornton, 2009–2010, will appear in the text.

24 "People Who Do Things," no page, undated clipping, Thornton family collection. Unless otherwise indicated, all identified, unidentified and undated magazine and newspaper clippings are from the Thornton family collection and cited in the endnotes as magazine clipping or newspaper clipping.

25 "A Letter from Mrs. M. V. Thornton," *Regina Leader-Post,* August 12, 1932

26 Farr, *J.W. Beatty,* p. 15

27 J.W. Beatty, "A Canadian Painter and His Work" *The Canadian Magazine,* (April 1906), p. 546, as quoted in Farr, p. 44

28 "Canadian Artist to Address Club," newspaper clipping

29 J.M. Thornton, "Mildred Valley Thornton," p. 1

30 Thornton, unpublished "Foreword," p. 6

31 Bumsted, *History of the Canadian Peoples,* p. 204

32 J.M. Thornton, "Mildred Valley Thornton," p. 1

33 Thornton, *Indian Lives and Legends,* pp. VII–VIII

34 Robert Francis, "She Treks Thousands of Miles to Paint Indian Life," *Toronto Star Weekly,* November 22, 1947

35 Kenneth Lochhead of the Regina College of Art (1926–2006) was one of the renowned Regina Five in the '60s. He started the well-known Emma Lake Artists Workshop, and B.C. artists Jack Shadbolt (1909–1998) and Joe Plaskett (born in 1918) were some of the first guests.

36 Ken Mitchell, "Arts and Culture," *Encyclopedia of Saskatchewan,* accessed September 8, 2010, http://esask.uregina .ca/entry/arts_and_culture

37 "Milestones and Memories," *Regina Leader-Post,* September 24, 1934

38 Jack Thornton to Anthony Westbridge, April 24, 1989, Westbridge Fine Art, Thornton Archive

39 J.M. Thornton, "Family Background," p. 2

40 Unofficial copy of "Registration Card" from the Art Institute of Chicago, courtesy of Matthew Sams, Assistant Director, Registration & Records, School of the Art Institute of Chicago

41 "People Who Do Things," magazine clipping

42 "Women's Art Association Hears Interesting Paper by Mrs. J.H. Thornton" *Regina Leader-Post,* November 14, 1929

43 Mitchell, "Arts and Culture"

44 "Historical Pictures to Feature Annual Exhibit by Mrs. J.H. Thornton," April 12, 1930, newspaper clipping

45 "Bryant Opens Art Exhibit," newspaper clipping

46 Circa 1950s, Mildred painted a portrait of Tilly Rolston, the first female MLA in British Columbia. In 1948, she had unsuccessfully proposed undertaking the portrait of then B.C. Premier "Duff" Pattullo as part of a historical collection of premiers' portraits.

47 Letter from Cowan to Thornton, June 21, 1934, Thornton family collection

48 "Glowing Color Distinguishing Quality of Mrs. Thornton's Work," newspaper clipping

49 Ibid.

50 "Regina Artist's Work Receives Recognition," March 18, 1933, newspaper clipping

51 There is the possibility that the following three titles, *In the Touchwood Hills, Saskatchewan, The Touchwood Hills* and *Evening at Touchwood Hills, Saskatchewan,* refer to the same image or variations of the same image. What the author has verified is that the painting in the National Gallery of Canada, *The Touchwood Hills,* is dated circa 1930 and *Evening at Touchwood Hills, Saskatchewan* (p. 103 of *Buffalo People*) is dated circa 1920. The title *In the Touchwood Hills, Saskatchewan* can be found in newspaper

articles and in Evelyn de R. McMann's *Royal Canadian Academy of Arts/Académie royale des arts du Canada: Exhibitions and Members 1880–1979,* Toronto: University of Toronto Press, 1981, p. 402.

52 According to the "Catalogue of the Fifty-Fifth Exhibition of the Royal Canadian Academy of Arts," November 1934, *Foreclosed* was priced at $600 and *Bulwarks of the Prairie* was priced at $300; catalogue courtesy of Sandra Bell, Reference Services, Library and Archives Canada. In 1941, Mildred exhibited the portrait of Dominic Jack, priced at $200.

53 E-mail from Charlie Hill (Curator of Canadian Art, National Gallery of Canada) to Mona Fertig, January 17, 2011; courtesy of Mona Fertig

54 "Saskatchewan Artists Are Sending Paintings to Toronto for C.N.E.," *Regina Leader-Post,* July 18, 1930

55 Ibid.

56 John Vanderpant to Norman Hacking, "Cabbages and Cameras," *Vancouver Province,* November 30, 1935

57 "Over $350 Is Received from Art Exhibit," *Regina Daily Post,* newspaper clipping

CHAPTER TWO: AN ARTIST THROUGH AND THROUGH

1 Thornton, unpublished manuscript, 1; 5. In one draft, the manuscript is titled "Tom Thomson," and "Pathways to Painting" in another; Thornton family collection.

2 Ibid., p. 6

3 Author's telephone interview with Mildred's niece, Audrey Stinson, February 5, 2010

4 Lara T. Evoy, "Cross-Cultural Relationships: The Work of Canadian Artist Mildred Valley Thornton," master's thesis, Concordia University, 1999, 56, accessed April 28, 2009, http://spectrum.library.concordia.ca/915/1/MQ43678.pdf

5 Ashwell, "Mildred Valley Thornton," p. 30

6 According to Jack Thornton, a church minister befriended Mildred and then borrowed several of her journals. They were never returned.

7 Diaries of D.A. MacLean, May 23, 1931, courtesy of the MacLean Family. Unless otherwise indicated, all further references to MacLean's Diaries will be cited in the text.

8 Ibid., June 8, 1931

9 Author's telephone interview with Katheryn (MacLean) Broughton, February 17, 2010

10 Margaret MacLean in an e-mail to the author from James Broughton, March 12, 2010

11 Katheryn Broughton in an e-mail from James Broughton to Mark Reid (*The Beaver*), January 27, 2010, courtesy of Shay Wilson

12 Broughton, February 17, 2010

13 "Glowing Color Distinguishing Quality," newspaper clipping

14 Broughton, February 17, 2010

15 Ibid.

16 Ibid. J.M. (Jack) Thornton published numerous pen-and-ink sketches in the Royal Canadian Navy chronicle, *Crowsnest* (1948–1965), and two books: *Warships 1860–1970: A Collection of Naval Lore* (Vancouver: Douglas David and Charles), 1973 and *Men-Of-War 1770–1970* (Hertfordshire: Argus Books), 1978. He also compiled a collection of twelve pen-and-ink sketches of the Vancouver area titled "Columbia Collection." W.M. (Maitland) Thornton published several publications on the subject of militaria, including two books: *Militaria* (Singapore: Kyodo Printing Co.), 2009, and *Submarine Insignia & Submarine Services of the World* (U.S. Naval Institute Press), 1997. According to Jack, Maitland was a militiaria consultant for a number of films, including *The Dirty Dozen*.

17 Broughton, February 17, 2010

CHAPTER THREE: A VERY ENTHUSIASTIC WOMAN

1 "Milestones and Memories," newspaper clipping

2 "Woman Artist Back from East," newspaper clipping

3 "Breezelets," *West End Breeze* (Vancouver), III, no. 13, May 16, 1935, Thornton family collection

4 Canadian Pacific Railway menu, private collection. During the 1920s and 1930s, the work of noted Canadian artists was featured on Canadian Pacific Railway menus, including W.J. Phillips and Nicholas de Grandmaison.

5 "Mission Statement," Soroptimist Club, accessed July 26, 2010 http://www.wcsoroptimist.org/clubs/clubs%20-%20vancouver.html

6 Mildred Valley Thornton, "B.C. Artists Evading War's Responsibility," *Vancouver Sun,* September 26, 1942

7 Elizabeth O'Kiely, *The Arts and Our Town: The Community Arts Council of Vancouver 1946–1996,*

Vancouver: The Community Arts Council of
Vancouver, 1996

8   Author's telephone interview with Frank Wade,
November 26, 2009. During the 1940s and 1950s,
the members of the B.C. writing community
included Christie Harris, Malcolm Lowry,
William McConnell (founder of Klanak Press),
Ethel Wilson and George Woodcock.

9   Vancouver Poetry Society, Add. MSS Loc.
526–E–1, file 3

10 City of Vancouver Archives, (hereafter CVA) Add.
MSS 294 Loc. 526–D–5, file 2

11 Ibid.

12 Ibid.

13 CVA, Add. MSS 294, Loc. 526–D–5, file 2

14 Ibid.

15 CVA, Add.MSS 294, Loc. 526–E–1, file 2

16 The Lyric West radio programme ended in 1945
and resumed briefly in 1946.

17 CVA, Add. MSS 294, Loc. 526–E–3, file 6. Some
of the other VPS members who participated in
The Lyric West were Dr. Ernest Fewster, May
Judge, Dorothy Livesay, Duncan MacNair, Mary
Matheson and Al Purdy.

18 Ibid., Add.MSS 294, Loc. 526–D–5, file 6

19 Ibid., Add.MSS 294, Loc. 526–E–3, file 6

20 John Murray Gibbon to Thornton, December
18, 1942, Thornton private collection. In July
of 1946, Mildred participated in the Vancouver
Art Gallery's Jubilee Exhibition with Fred
Amess, Peter Aspell, Emily Carr, Arthur
Erikson, Lawren Harris, Beatrice Lennie, Vera
Mortimer-Lamb, Joe Plaskett, Gordon Smith and
many others.

21 CVA, Vancouver Museum and Planetarium,
Totem-Land Society Correspondence, 1954, Add.
MSS 396, Loc. 547–C–7, File 6

22 Phil Nuytten, The Totem Carvers Charlie James,
Ellen Neel, and Mungo Martin, Vancouver:
Panorama Publications Ltd., 1982, pp. 47, 48

23 Ibid., p. 57

24 Ibid., pp. 51, 53

25 Untitled photograph caption, Vancouver Sun,
August 4, 1954, newspaper clipping

26 Thornton, "Indian Designs Go Modern,"
Vancouver Sun, June 29, 1946

27 Ellen Neel, University of British Columbia
Address, April 1948, as quoted in Nuytten, The
Totem Carvers, p. 50

28 Thornton, "Carver Ellen Neel Mourned," Native
Voice, xx, no. 20 (February 1966)

29 Note from A.M. Stephen to Mildred Valley
Thornton, February 8, 1941, Thornton family
collection

30 Sharon Fortney, "Entwined Histories: The
Creation of the Maisie Hurley Collection of
Native Art," BC Studies (Autumn 2010), p. 44

31 Thomas R. Berger, "Rap of a Cane and a Time
of Change," Law Alumni Magazine (Winter
2008), University of British Columbia, p.
6, accessed September 20, 2010, http://
www.law.ubc.ca/files/pdf/news/2008/feb/
Alumni_Mag_winter08pdf

32 Fortney, "Entwined Histories," p. 33

33 Vancouver News-Herald, December 27, 1951,
newspaper clipping; Fortney, "Entwined
Histories," p. 43

34 Newspacket: Newspaper of the Canadian Women's
Press Club, 30, no. 1 (November 1967), p. 1,
Thornton family collection

35 CVA, Canadian Women's Press Club, Add.
MSS 396, Loc. 554–C–1, file 2, "Scrapbook
1950–1958," p. 56

36 Ibid., Pat Wallace, "How It All Began," p. 32

37 Ibid., "Scrapbook 1965–1969," p. 14

38 Myrtle Gregory, Newspacket, (November 1967),
p. 13

39 Myrtle Gregory to Jack Thornton, November
1967, Thornton family collection

40 Author's e-mail correspondence with Kim
Svendsen, Assistant Registrar, Vancouver
Art Gallery, April 19, 2010. Willie Seaweed
was exhibited in This Place: Works from the
Collection (June 29, 2002–June 1, 2003); 75
Years of Collecting: First Nations Myths and
Realities (May 27–August 2006); and, Canadian
Women Modernists: the Dialogue with Emily
Carr (April 19–October 19, 2008)

CHAPTER FOUR: BUCKSKIN AND ADVOCACY

1   Thornton, Indian Lives and Legends, pp. VIII, IX

2   Ibid., pp. IX, XI, IX

3   Ibid., p. X

4   Ibid.

5   Mervyn Johns, "Owas-ka-ta-esk-ean," (published
elsewhere as "Owas-ka-esk-ean," Vancouver Daily
Province, Magazine Section, May 21, 1949

6   "Artist to Address Club," unidentified, undated
newspaper clipping

7   Thornton, unpublished, undated writings,
Thornton family collection

8   *Prince Albert Daily Herald,* March 7, 1947

9   "Pleads Cause of Indians with Fellow Canadians,"
    London Free Press, March 27, 1947

10 For many years, an oil painting of Mildred's
    titled *Jervis Inlet* (date unknown) hung in
    the Royal Suite of the Hotel Vancouver. The
    painting's whereabouts is currently unknown.

11 Letter from Ashwell to L.J. Wallace, April 27,
    1965, GR-1738, Box 148, file 26, B.C. Archives

12 Evoy, "Cross-Cultural Relationships," p. 89

13 Author's interview with Deborah Jacobs,
    May 27, 2009

14 Evoy, "Cross-Cultural Relationships, p. 41

15 Daniel Francis, *The Imaginary Indian: The Image
    of the Indian in Canadian Culture,* Vancouver:
    Arsenal Pulp Press, 1992, p. 21

16 See Francis, *The Imaginary Indian,* for a
    thorough discussion of this topic.

17 Alex Brass, "Regina Indians answer criticisms
    of their race; urge education, mixing," *Regina
    Leader-Post,* September 29, 1956

18 Thornton, "Indians And TB," *The Star Weekly,*
    1946, newspaper clipping

19 Thornton, "Indian Aristocracy," *Vancouver Sun
    Magazine Supplement,* November 25, 1950

20 Thornton, "Totems Fall, But Haidas Thrive,"
    Vancouver Sun Magazine Supplement,
    January 31, 1948

21 Ibid.

22 Thornton, "Indian Native Art," *Museum and Art
    Notes,* Art, Historical and Scientific Association
    of Vancouver, B.C., 1, no. 1 (September 1949), pp.
    22, 23–24, courtesy of Steven Lunsford

23 Thornton, "B.C. Indians Go Modern," *Vancouver
    Sun Magazine Supplement,* May 20, 1950

24 Thornton, "'Tzinquaw' B.C.'s Indian Drama,"
    Native Voice (December, 1950), p. 5. A similar
    article, "B.C.'s Indian Drama," appeared in the
    Vancouver Sun Magazine Supplement,
    June 24, 1950.

25 "They Tell Me," Claire Wallace, interviewer, CBC
    Radio, March 21, 1947

26 Author's interview with Deborah Jacobs,
    May 27, 2009

27 Letter from Dan Kennedy to Mildred Valley
    Thornton, May 21, 1947, Thornton family
    collection

28 Author's telephone interview with Lance Evoy,
    January 21, 2009

29 Augustus Brindle, "Vancouver Woman Artist
    Authority on Indian Life," newspaper clipping

30 Thornton, unpublished lecture notes

31 "'We Owe Much to Indians' Critic Tells Canadian
    Club," *Port-Arthur News-Chronicle,* March 15,
    1947

32 *Native Voice,* XIV, no. 10 (October 1960), clipping
    file

33 Thornton unpublished lecture notes

34 Evoy, "Cross-Cultural Relationships," p. 131

CHAPTER FIVE: CAPTURING A PAGE OF HISTORY

1   Shearer West, *Portraiture,* Oxford: Oxford
    University Press, 2004, p. 165

2   Thornton, *Potlatch People,* p. 11

3   Thornton, *Indian Lives and Legends,* p. XIII

4   Thornton, unpublished "Introduction," p. 7

5   Thornton, *Indian Lives and Legends,* p. XIII

6   Thornton, *Buffalo People,* p. 32

7   Thornton draft of letter to Marius Barbeau,
    August 1, 1965, Thornton family collection

8   Thornton, *Buffalo People,* p. 32

9   Thornton, unpublished "Introduction," p. 11

10 Ashwell, "Tribute to a lady." Reg passed away in
    September 2010.

11 Jimmy John was a master carver who died
    in 1986 at the age of 114. He was a direct
    descendent of Chief Maquinna of the Nuu-chah-
    nulth people, who first greeted Captain Cook.

12 Ashwell, "Tribute to a lady."

13 Ibid.

14 Author's interview with Reg Ashwell,
    March 3, 2009

15 Ashwell, "Tribute to a lady."

16 Jill Pollack, "Artist's historical importance
    outweighs her artistic impact," *Vancouver
    Courier,* November 7, 1990

17 Author's telephone interview with Gunter
    Heinrich, March 9, 2010

18 Author's interview with Uno Langmann
    October 23, 2009

19 Author's interview with Vanessa Campbell,
    May 27, 2009

20 Thornton, *Potlatch People,* pp. 121–123

21 Ibid., pp. 76–77

22 Author's interview with Margaret Locke,
    December 3, 2009

23 Thornton, *Potlatch People,* p. 181

24 Locke, December 3, 2009

25 Thornton, *Potlatch People,* pp. 181, 182

26 Locke, December 3, 2009

27 Thornton, *Potlatch People,* pp. 196–197

28 Ibid., p. 212

29 Ibid., p. 213

30 Thornton, unpublished writings

31 May P. Judge, "And Now Their Altar Is Complete," newspaper clipping

32 Thornton, *Potlatch People*, p. 309. The whereabouts of the portrait is currently unknown, but a photograph of the image is available on page 10 of the September 3, 1959, issue of the *Family Herald*.

33 Thornton, unpublished writings

34 Mildred misspelled the ancestor's name as "Paytsmauk." At the time, the Squamish Nation did not have an official writing system.

35 Vanessa Campbell, May 27, 2009

36 Author's communication with Anthony Westbridge, 2009–2010. Unless otherwise indicated, all further references to the author's communications with Westbridge will appear in the text.

37 Kw'achmixwáylh: Showing of the Pictures: Mildred Valley Thornton Collection of Squamish Nation Ancestors' Portraits, West Vancouver Museum, 1999

38 Ibid.

39 Jacobs, March 6, 2009

40 Ibid.

41 Campbell, March 6, 2009

42 Ibid.

43 Ibid.

44 J.L. Homan to Thornton from February 21, 1958, Thornton family collection

45 Jennifer Kramer, *Switchbacks: Art, Ownership, and Nuxalk National Identity*, Vancouver: UBC Press, 2006, pp. 76–77

46 Westbridge is currently preparing a *catalogue raisonné* of Mildred's First Nations portraits, forthcoming in 2011.

CHAPTER SIX: AN INDOMITABLE SPIRIT

1 Ashwell, March 3, 2009

2 Ashwell, "Tribute to a lady"

3 Thornton, *Potlatch People*, pp. 115–117

4 Ashwell, "Tribute to a lady"

5 Ibid.

6 Ibid.

7 Jack Thornton and his friend Frank Kennedy photographed all of Mildred's portrait collection, many of her scenes of aboriginal life and activities and some landscapes.

8 Ashwell, "Tribute to a lady"

9 Ashwell, March 3, 2009

10 Ashwell, "Tribute to a lady"

11 Mildred Valley Thornton, "Hazardous Journey," unpaginated, unpublished story

12 Jan Gould, *Women of British Columbia*, Saanichton, B.C.: Hancock House, 1975, p. 194

13 Douglas Cole and Christine Mullins, "'Haida Ida': The Musical World of Ida Halpern," *BC Studies*, no. 97 (Spring 1993), p. 33

14 Thornton, *Potlatch People*, pp. 259–260

15 Ibid., pp. 262–264

16 Ibid., pp. 265; 266

17 Ibid., pp. 56–57

18 Ibid., pp. 93–94, 96

19 Ibid., pp. 231; 234

20 Thornton, *Buffalo People*, p. 184

21 In 1990, Patricia Richardson Logie published *Chronicles of Pride: A Journey of Discovery*, Calgary, Detselig Enterprises. The book features 31 portraits of Canadian First Nations individuals that Logie began in 1982. She donated the portrait collection to the University of British Columbia in 2009.

22 Flora Kyle, Interest Growing In B.C. Indian Art," *Vancouver Sun*, March 10, 1961

CHAPTER SEVEN: A GUTSY ARTIST

1 Author's telephone interview with Ian Sigvaldason, February 19, 2010

2 Author's interview with an anonymous private collector, January 19, 2010

3 John Vanderpant as quoted in Sheryl Salloum's *Underlying Vibrations: The Photography and Life of John Vanderpant*, Victoria: Horsdal & Schubart, 1995, pp. 49–50

4 Ibid., pp. 47–48

5 Thornton, *Potlatch People*, p. 261

6 Salloum, *Underlying Vibrations*, p. 50

7 Author's interview with Gordon Smith, September 15, 2010

8 Emily Carr, *Hundreds and Thousands: The Journals of Emily Carr*, Toronto: Clarke, Irwin & Co., 1966, p. 330

9 Originally, Mary Elizabeth Colman, in "Painter of Indian Life," *Native Voice*, (December 1950), p. 7, described Mildred as "North American as hard wheat." Over the years, those words have been misquoted by others as "Canadian as hard wheat."

10 Prakash, *Independent Spirits*, p. 25

11   Smith, September 15, 2010

12   L. Johanne Stemo, "The Indians Call Her"Owas-ka-ta-esk-ean," *Family Herald,* September 3, 1959

13   "'No-Jury' B.C. Show Triumph for Artists," *Vancouver Sun,* September 25, 1943

14   Prakash, *Independent Spirits,* p. 30

15   Thornton, "New Emily Carr Show at Gallery," *Vancouver Sun,* June 16, 1943

16   "Tuesday Night ca. 22 June 1943," in *Corresponding Influences: Selected Letters of Emily Carr and Ira Dilworth,* ed. Linda Morra, Toronto: University of Toronto Press, 2006, p. 209

17   Thornton, "Art Exhibit Demonstrates True Talent of Emily Carr," *Vancouver Sun,* May 8, 1946

18   Thornton, unpublished writings, Thornton family collection

19   Langmann, October 23, 2009

20   Memorandum from Wilson Dull to C.G. Carl, Gr-1738, June 21, 1965, Box 148, File 26, B. C. Archives

Chapter Eight: A Big Statement

1   Author's telephone interview with Jo Rappaport, June 18, 2009

2   Langmann, October 23, 2009

3   Ibid.

4   Ibid.

5   Letter from Ashwell to Jack Thornton, November 18, 1970, Thornton family collection

6   Author's telephone interview with Alison Bridger, April 9, 2010

7   *Seattle Post Intelligencer,* circa 1940, as quoted in "City Artist's Work Praised in Seattle," *Vancouver Province,* July 16, 1940, newspaper clipping

8   Interview with Unity Bainbridge, March 17, 2009

9   Letters from B.C. Binning to Thornton, March 9, 1944; Alyce Shearer, March 13, 1944; Jack G. Nilan, August 11, 1941, Thornton family collection

10   Jill Pollack, "Trying to Clutch Water," *STEP* (May/June 1991), p. 97

11   G. Van Houghten, *Vancouver Daily Herald,* 1939, as quoted in Jill Pollack, "Trying to Clutch Water," p. 98

12   Thornton, "Modern Art," *Canadian Spectator* (April 18, 1936), magazine clipping

13   Thornton, "Vancouver's Art Gallery Oasis of Beauty, Vision," *Vancouver Sun,* August 24, 1940

14   Pollack, "Trying to Clutch Water," p. 99

15   Scott Watson, "Art in the Fifties Design, Leisure, and Painting in the Age of Anxiety," in *Vancouver Art and Artists 1931–1983,* Vancouver: Vancouver Art Gallery, 1983, p. 73

16   *The Arts and Our Town,* eds. Community Arts Survey Committee, Vancouver: Keystone Press, 1946, p. 39

17   *The People,* 3, no. 26, (July 1, 1944), p. 7, as quoted in Watson, "Art in the Fifties," p. 72

18   Watson, "Art in the Fifties," p. 101

19   *Vancouver Art Gallery Bulletin,* 12, no. 1 (September 1944), p. 4

20   Frank Molnar, "Let's Get Rid of Our Artistic Snobbery," letter to the editor, *Vancouver Province,* November 12, 1962

21   "Artist Rebels Open Own Show," *Vancouver Sun,* October 17, 1944

22   Thornton, "Labour Arts Guild Shows How Exhibition Can Succeed," *Vancouver Sun,* November 23, 1944. Some of the artists who participated in the 1944 and 1945 British Columbia at Work exhibitions included Alister Bell, Nan Lawson Cheney, Molly Lamb Bobak, Jack Shadbolt, Lionel Thomas and Ina D.D. Uhthoff.

23   Thornton, "B.C. Artists 'Imitators' Says Critic," *Vancouver Sun,* September 23, 1947

24   Thornton, "Odd Anatomy in Art Show," *Vancouver Sun,* October 27, 1944

25   Thornton, "City Man's Work Now at Gallery," *Vancouver Sun,* November 6, 1957

26   Author's telephone interview with Marya Fiamengo, December 1, 2010

27   Smith, September 15, 2010

28   Some B.C. artists in the exhibition were Fred Amess, Peter Aspell, B.C. Binning, Bruno Bobak, Molly Lamb Bobak, Sonia Cornwall, George Fertig, Bess Harris, Lawren Harris, E.J. Hughes, L. Petley-Jones, Vera Mortimer-Lamb, J.A.S. MacDonald, David Marshall, Irene Hoffar-Reid, Jack Shadbolt, Gordon Smith, Lionel Thomas, Gordon Kit Thorne and Ina D.D. Uhthoff.

29   Thornton, "Outstanding Paintings in Watercolor Exhibit," *Vancouver Sun,* December 8, 1950

30   Thornton, "Good, Bad Paintings Displayed at Gallery," *Vancouver Sun,* December 2, 1950

31   Lawren Harris, "Sun Critic Doesn't Understand Idea of New Art Exhibition," letter to the editor, *Vancouver Sun,* December 8, 1950

32   Letter to the editor, *Vancouver Sun,* December 21, 1950

33   Molly Lamb Bobak, letter to the editor, *Vancouver*

34 *Sun,* December 21, 1950
    M. Denton-Burgess, undated letter to the editor, *Vancouver Sun,* VAG clipping files

35 Burgess, "'The Other Side of the Picture' in the Art Gallery Controversy," , *Vancouver Sun,* 1950, VAG clipping files

36 Smith, September 15, 2010

37 Thornton, "Expressionist Paintings on Exhibition," *Vancouver Sun,* January 29, 1950

38 Watson, "Art in the Fifties," p. 90

39 Thornton, "Art for the Arty Current Trend at Vancouver Gallery," *Vancouver Sun,* February 24, 1951

40 Mac Reynolds, "Art Dictatorship Charged by Critic," *Vancouver Sun,* December 13, 1951

41 Transcript of videotaped interview of Jack Shadbolt by Dorothy Metcalfe, August 25, 1974, p. 15, Jack Shadbolt file 1980–1989, Vancouver Art Gallery Library

42 Transcript of Ted Lindberg interview with Jack Shadbolt, August 1980, p. 26, Jack Shadbolt file 1980–1989, Vancouver Art Gallery Library

43 Smith, September 15, 2010

44 Jack Shadbolt, "Thank God for Artistic Experimenters, Says Top B.C. Artist," *Vancouver Sun,* January 15, 1952

45 "B.C. Art Best in Canada but Where Is It Hidden?" *Vancouver Sun,* February 6, 1960

46 Ashwell, March 3, 2009

47 When asked to comment on Mildred's work for this publication, in a January 14, 2010 e-mail to the author, Ian Thom, the senior curator, historical, at the Vancouver Art Gallery said he does not know enough about Mildred's art to be able to comment.

48 "Sun Art Critic Assisted at Exhibit," *Vancouver Sun,* July 15, 1958

49 CVA, Women's Press Club, Add.MSS 396, Loc. 554–C–1, file 2, "Scrapbook 1950–1958," p. 24

50 *Oakridge Shopping Centre News,* June 12, 1962, Thornton family collection

CHAPTER NINE: STEPPING OUTSIDE THE NORM

1 Kathy Hassard, "Something to Suit Every Artistic Taste," *Vancouver Sun,* December 17, 1966

2 Author's telephone interview with Leonard Woods, March 30, 2009

3 Ibid.

4 Mona Fertig, *The Life and Art of George Fertig,*

    Salt Spring Island: Mother Tongue Publishing, 2010, p. 95

5 Author's communications with Danny Kostyshin, April 7, 2009; April 8, 2009

6 Author's telephone interview with Eric Schou Hamerum, October 8, 2009

7 Mona Fertig interview with Eric Schou Hammerum, November 16, 2007; courtesy of Mona Fertig

8 The Silk Purse Gallery does not have a record of lectures for that time period.

9 E-mail to author from David Stouck, February 20, 2010

10 Pollack, "Artist's Historical Importance Outweighs Her Artistic Impact," *Vancouver Courier,* November 7, 1990

11 Maria Tippett, *By a Lady: Celebrating Three Centuries of Art by Canadian Women,* Toronto: Penguin Books, 1992. Five years after Tippett's book was published, Thornton was listed as one of B.C.'s "significant artists" in Tony Robertson's "Artists of Greater Vancouver: The First Three Generations," in Chuck Davis's *The Greater Vancouver Book: An Urban Encyclopedia,* Surrey: Linkman Press, 1997, p. 652.

12 E-mail from Brooks Joyner to author, June 1, 2009. Brooks Joyner is the Director of the Allentown Art Museum, in Pennsylvania.

13 Brooks Joyner to Anthony Westbridge, June 27, 1994, Westbridge Fine Art Thornton Archive

14 Ibid.

15 E-mail from Brooks Joyner to author, June 1, 2009

16 E-mail from Eva Major-Marothy to author, December 24, 2009

17 Author's telephone interview with anonymous American collector, June 2010

18 Author's telephone interviews with Christian Cardell Corbet, 2009

19 Ibid.

CHAPTER TEN: PASSIONATE AND INCOMPARABLE

1 Author's telephone interview with John Thornton, May 3, 2009

2 Author's interview with Phyllis Thornton, April 14, 2009

3 John Thornton, May 3, 2009

4 Thornton to Barry Mather, May 18, 1967, University of British Columbia Library, University Archives, Norman MacKenzie Fonds,

Mildred Valley Thornton Correspondence, Box 202–19

5   John Thornton, May 3, 2009

6   Thornton, "Indians of British Columbia," *Journal of the Royal Society of Arts*, CVIII, no. 5043 (February 1960), pp. 211–226

7   Ibid., p. 224

8   Ibid., pp. 221; 222

9   Thornton to W.E. Ireland, March 8, 1949, Correspondence 1910–1976, Gr–1738, Box 148, file 26, B.C. Archives

10 Personal recollection of author who taught public school in the Cariboo-Chilcotin School District

11 "Interdepartmental Memorandum" from Dr. H.B. Hawthorn to Norman Mackenzie, July 18, 1956, Audrey and Harry Hawthorn Library and Archives, Museum of Anthropology (MOA), Vancouver, Canada, Audrey Hawthorn Fonds, Box 12–5, file 5–B–77.

12 Alwyne Buckley to Norman Mackenzie, July 15, 1958, Audrey and Harry Hawthorn Library and Archives, MOA, Vancouver, Canada, Audrey Hawthorn Fonds, Box 12–5, file 5–B–77

13 Dr. H.B. Hawthorn to Norman Mackenzie, August 6, 1958, Audrey and Harry Hawthorn Library and Archives, MOA, Vancouver, Canada, Audrey Hawthorn Fonds, Box 12–5, file 5–B–77

14 Ian McNairn to Norman Mackenzie, August 8, 1958, Harry Hawthorn Fonds, Box 11–46, University of British Columbia Archives

15 The Mildred Valley Thornton Memorial Scholarship (1985–2006) was one of sixty President's Regional Entrance Scholarships named after B.C. individuals of historical significance. The scholarships were discontinued in 2008.

16 Dr. H.B. Hawthorn to Norman Mackenzie, May 29, 1961, Audrey and Harry Hawthorn Library and Archives, MOA, Vancouver, Canada, Audrey Hawthorn Fonds, Box 12–5, file 5–B–77

17 Mildred Valley Thornton draft letter to Hon. Wesley Black, July 15, 1963, Thornton family collection

18 Ibid., September 5, 1964

19 Mildred Valley Thornton draft letter to L.J. Wallace, August 12, 1964, Thornton family collection

20 Ibid., September 21, 1964

21 Ibid., undated draft letter

22 Mildred Valley Thornton, August 1, 1965 letter to Marius Barbeau, Thornton family collection.

23 Mildred Valley Thronton, undated draft letter to Marius Barbeau, Thornton Family Collection

24 Reg Ashwell to L.J. Wallace, April 27, 1965, Correspondence 1910–1976, Gr–1738, Box 148, file 26, B.C. Archives

25 Memorandum from Wilson Duff to Dr. G.C. Carl, June 21, 1965, Gr–1738, Box 148, file 26, B.C. Archives

26 Dr. W. Wymond's account of Johnny Chickite's initiation ceremony was published in 1914 in *Stories of Early British Columbia,* Vancouver: *Vancouver News-Advertiser,* and has been partly retold in Jeanette Taylor's book, *The Quadra Story: A History of Quadra Island,* Madeira Park, B.C.: Harbour Publishing, 2009.

27 Memorandum from Wilson Duff to Dr. G.C. Carl, June 21, 1965, Gr-1738, Box 148, file 26, B.C. Archives

28 W.E. Ireland to Thornton, September 23, 1965, Gr-1738, Box 148, file 26, B.C. Archives

29 Draft letter from Thornton to L.J. Wallace, September 25, 1965, Gr-1738, Box 148, file 26, B.C. Archives

30 Letter from Thornton to W.E. Ireland, October 15, 1965, Gr-1738, Box 148, file 26, B.C. Archives

31 Ibid.

32 M.Y. Williams to Hon. Wesley Black, June 18, 1965, Gr-1738, Box 148, file 26, B.C. Archives

33 Thornton undated rough draft letter to John MacAuley, Thornton family collection

34 Thornton rough draft of letter to John MacAuley, July 30, 1965, Thornton family collection

35 Undated draft letter from Thornton to Mr. Bennett (possibly Premier W.A.C. Bennett), Thornton family collection

36 Thornton undated rough drafts of letters to the curator of the Mendel Art Gallery and Dr. Rogers, curator of the Royal Ontario Museum. Thornton also wrote the curator of the Pion-era Museum, Saskatchewan, June 22, 1965.

37 Mildred Valley Thornton to Barry Mather, May 18, 1967, University of British Columbia Library, University Archives, Norman MacKenzie Fonds, Mildred Valley Thornton Correspondence, Box 202–19

38 Norman Mackenzie to Barry Mather, May 29, 1967, University of British Columbia Library, University Archives, Norman MacKenzie Fonds, Mildred Valley Thornton Correspondence, Box 202–19

39 Barry Mather to Mildred Valley Thornton, University of British Columbia Library, University Archives, Norman MacKenzie Fonds, Mildred Valley Correspondence, Box 202–19

40 Barry Mather to L.J. Wallace, July 27, 1967, University of British Columbia Library, University Archives, Norman MacKenzie Fonds, Mildred Valley Thornton Correspondence, Box 202–19

41 Dr. H.B. Hawthorn to Norman MacKenzie, August 6, 1958, Audrey and Harry Hawthorn Library and Archives, MOA, Vancouver, Canada, Audrey Hawthorn Fonds, Box 12–5, B-77

42 Copy of codicil to Thornton's will, June 12, 1967, Thornton family collection

43 Letter from W.E. Ireland to Barry Mather, August 9, 1967, University of British Columbia Library, University Archives, Norman Mackenzie Fonds, Mildred Valley Thornton Correspondence, Box 202–19

44 Letter from Barry Mather to W.E. Ireland, August 15, 1967, University of British Columbia Library, University Archives, Norman Mackenzie Fonds, Mildred Valley Thornton Correspondence, Box 202–19

45 Norman Mackenzie to Barry Mather, August 25, 1967, University of British Columbia Library, University Archives, Norman Mackenzie Fonds, Box 202–19

46 Arthur Laing to Barry Mather, November 30, 1967, University of British Columbia Library, University Archives, Norman Mackenzie Fonds, Box 202–19. Laing also indicated that Mildred's collection had once been offered to the Provincial Museum for $10,000.

47 Norman Mackenzie to Barry Mather, December 11, 1967, University of British Columbia Library, University Archives, Norman Mackenzie Fonds, Box 202–19

48 Torben Kristiansen to Jack Thornton, January 1, 1972, as quoted in Lara T. Evoy, "Cross-Cultural Relationships," p. 125

49 Two examples are Chris Pettey's, *Dictionary of Women Artists: An International Dictionary of Women Artists Born Before 1900*, (Boston: G.K. Hall & Co. 1985); Marketa Newman, *Biographical Dictionary of Saskatchewan Artists: Women Artists* (Saskatoon: Fifth House Publishers, 1990).

⌐ Mildred on front porch with carving of blackfish
1959
THORNTON FAMILY
PRIVATE COLLECTION
IB MEYER-OBEL PHOTOGRAPHER

⌐ *Tsimshian Blackfish*
n. d., watercolour
10½" x 14½"
PRIVATE COLLECTION
JOHN CAMERON PHOTOGRAPHY

INDEX

Italicized page numbers refer to photos